Christy Morgan's *Character Development in Ch[rist* will]
help bring breakthrough for every born-again be[liever. If you have a his]-
tory from past hurts or ungodly thoughts and actions in your life, *Character Devel-*
opment in Christ will help you overcome these old patterns and bring transformation
into living in freedom as a new creation in Christ Jesus.

> *Deanne "Dee" Barnes*
> Founder, His Wonderful Works, Inc.
> CEO, Evans Tool & Die, Inc.
> Conyers, Georgia

As a Christian prayer counselor for over thirty years, I have found *Character Development in Christ* a must-read for everyone who desires healing and understanding from early root traumas and deprivations. This is a powerful account of Christy's healing journey achieved through her reliance and vulnerability upon Christ, His cross, resurrection power, and written Word.

She also demonstrates the power in speaking His Word repetitively out loud and explains the correlation between the kidneys and the *inmost mind* as a symbol of this process. As the kidneys remove toxic waste from the blood to keep the body healthy, in the same way, the *inmost mind*, as Christ's Words of truth spoken become a consistent flow, flushes out carnal untruths of the false self. Thus, the true self rises up out of the fallen mindset into a solid sense of our true identity found only in Christ Jesus.

> *Beverly Gammalo*
> Christian Prayer Counselor
> Stockbridge, Georgia

Character Development in Christ is a must-read for Christians that desire to grow closer to the Father. James 4:8 – *"Draw near to God, and he will draw near to you."* James tells us to draw near to God. Christy reveals practical ways to do this. She does so through sharing her personal healing and the steps to that healing. The continued healing of her soul and spirit take place as she is discipled by the Holy Spirit.

This is not only a great read, but it gives you practical steps for your life. The Scriptures that change lives are presented and developed so that Christians can walk in a new-found freedom and experience the abundant life of the believer.

As Christy's pastor for many years, I have watched as she has matured in Christ.

As this book details her adventure, she now lives and ministers from wholeness rather than hurt. Rather than simply reading the book, I encourage you to study it.

Eddie Mason
Senior Pastor
Southside Christian Fellowship Church
McDonough, Georgia

I dedicate this book

to my Lord and Savior, Jesus Christ,
who rescued me from myself and restored my soul
from deep-rooted insecurities to a new life in Him.
He has blessed me with a godly husband, Don,
and two beautiful children, Jonathan and Jessica.
I dedicate this book to Jesus Christ to give glory to Him
and to my heavenly Father who has made it possible
for all of us to live out of the born-again creation.

CONTENTS

Acknowledgements ix
Foreword xi

Introduction 1

1. Understanding Its Importance 5

2. My Story
    Part One 15
    Part Two 31

3. Don's Testimony 49

4. Personalized Scripture Guide
    Details and Directives 53
    Important Notice 65
    Part One
       Scriptures Designed to Help Put Off the Old Man Concerning:
       Cares and Anxieties of this World and Distractions of the Age 67
    Part Two
       Scriptures Designed to Help Put Off the Old Man Concerning:
       False Glamour, Deceitfulness of Riches, and the Craving and
       Passionate Desire for Other Things 77
    Part Three
       Scriptures Designed to Help Put Off the Old Man and Put On
       the New Man Concerning:
       A. Behavior Patterns and Mindsets 85
       B. Work Ethics, Submission to Authority, and Entering into
          His Sufferings 99
       C. Marriage 105
       D. Family 113

5. Personal Prayer Journal – From your heart to His
    Details and Instructions 119

    Part One
        Designed to Help Put Off the Old Man Concerning:
        Cares and Anxieties of This World and Distractions of the Age 127
    Part Two
        Designed to Help Put Off the Old Man Concerning:
        False Glamour, Deceitfulness of Riches, and the Craving and
        Passionate Desire for Other Things.. 139
    Part Three
        Designed to Help Put Off the Old Man Concerning:
        Behavior Patterns and Mindsets.. 151

6. Prayers of Repentance.. 163
    My Responsibility as a Wife 165
    My Responsibility as a Husband.. 166
    My Responsibility as a Mother 167
    My Responsibility as a Father 169

7. A Heart of Thanksgiving
    The Importance of Giving Thanks... 171
    A Heart of Thanksgiving Prayer Guide 175

Exhibits
    Exhibit A.. 179
    Exhibit B.. 180
    Exhibit C-1 181
    Exhibit C-2 182
    Exhibit D 183

Support and Help.. 189

Suggested Reading.. 190

Endnotes... 191

ACKNOWLEDGEMENTS

My special thanks to my husband, Don. You were there for me to read over material and provided the spiritual and mental support I needed throughout this work. Thank you for all the encouraging words and your much-needed strength.

My special thanks to my niece, Lisa Doolittle. You have been an inspiration and my greatest encourager throughout this project. I have called upon you many times for input and you have provided much needed wisdom and insight. You are a treasure.

My special thanks to our long-time friend Robert Moore. You have been so faithful in providing the much-needed technical support throughout the years while writing this book. Your help has been invaluable.

My special thanks to Ellah Mahan who created the beautiful painting that graces the cover of this book. You are a gift from God.

My special thanks to Dr. Su Mason. Along with your common sense and spiritual maturity, I appreciate how you graciously and methodically helped edit this book in its initial stages.

My special thanks to Katie Caron. You helped me by proofreading and making grammar and punctuation corrections where needed in its final stages. You typeset the book, prepared the cover, and all the other details prior to printing. Your professionalism, work ethics, and Christlike character was so refreshing to me and much appreciated.

Christy Morgan

FOREWORD

Christy Morgan has written one of the most needed and insightful books entitled, *Character Development in Christ*. The revelation of Christ is the Father's means to have a change of nature, transforming the inner being, the hidden places of the heart. This revelation is awakening with fresh understanding in the church worldwide. Her book, sound in doctrine, is written with scriptural foundation at every step, as she and her husband, Don, share honestly their own real life struggles. By their humble seeking to find merciful answers, they offer to others transparent help in experiencing His righteousness, in the secret places of one's conscience and thought life (Psalms 51:6). Christy's message is timely, as the Holy Spirit is bringing fresh emphasis upon the mystery of *"Christ in you the hope of glory."*

This book is very practical for everyone who desires godly character developing in their own life. Christy presents this, not in duty, but in joy, through finding amazing levels of the person of Christ resident in one's own heart. As she writes, understanding opens to how the *mind being renewed* empowers all who desire to rise in a consistency of godly character developed by experiencing who the living Christ is in them.

Chris Strong
Senior Pastor, Christ Fellowship
of Stone Mountain
Stone Mountain, Georgia

INTRODUCTION

The two main objectives of ***Character Development in Christ*** are (1) to reveal to the church the importance for every born-again believer to put off the old man, who we are "in Adam," our carnal nature, and to put on the new man, the born-again creation "in Christ," and (2) to be a vehicle to help others obtain this victory. Following is a brief description of the chapters:

<u>**Chapter**</u> <u>**Synopsis**</u>

1. *Understanding Its Importance* – Introducing the prophecy, how it applied in my life, and how it can impact your life.

2. *My Story – Part One and Two* – I share detailed accounts of the Lord's mercy and grace throughout my life, and the victory I have obtained through putting off the old man and putting on the new man.

3. *Don's Testimony* – My husband's very moving and powerful testimony of God's amazing love and grace in his life.

4. *Personalized Scripture Guide* – The heart of ***Character Development in Christ*** as most chapters revolve around it (including the ***Scripture Guide Study Notes - Volume 2***). It is divided into fifty portions of Scripture and each portion of Scripture includes "words of wisdom" from the Lord entitled *Heart-to-heart*. It is separated into three parts and designed to help you put off the old man and put on the new man in Christ.

5. *Personal Prayer Journal – From your heart to His* – This prayer journal is also separated into three parts, which coincide with the sections of the Scripture guide.

6. *Prayers of Repentance* – Prayers to help guide you through the act of repentance as wives, husbands, mothers, and fathers.

7. *A Heart of Thanksgiving* – The importance of giving thanks to the Lord, offering up thanksgiving and prayers for others, and a Heart of Thanksgiving Prayer Guide to help.

Character Development in Christ, through the renewal process, is designed to help born-again believers put off the old man, by removing anything in one's heart and mind that may be hindering the new man from becoming a reality (John 3:3; 1 Peter 1:23; Hebrews 4:12-13; Romans 12:1-2; Ephesians 4:20-24). The only way to live a victorious life is to live out of this new man, or as 1 Peter 3:4 describes it, *"The hidden man of the heart."* This is the true meaning of life, and what I believe Paul is referring to, which reads,

> *The mystery which has been hidden from ages and from generations but now has been revealed to His saints. To them God willed to make known what are the riches of the glory of this <u>mystery</u> among the Gentiles: <u>which is Christ in you, the hope of glory</u>.*
>
> (Colossians 1:26-27, NKJV)

This new way of living is not dependent on life's circumstances, nor on what we think or feel, but rather on God's truth being made a reality within us in order to live by faith and not by sight, trusting our heavenly Father in every situation and circumstance of life (2 Corinthians 4:17-18). God's desire is that every member of the body of Christ live out of this new creation by putting on the new man, and **Character Development in Christ** is designed to help you do just that.

In ***My Story – Part One***, I share in detail, how I obtained freedom in Christ from living a lifestyle of homosexuality for thirteen years, which is a product of the old man, truly believing that I was born that way at the age of six. I also share how core beliefs that formed during my childhood years had a negative impact in the way that I perceived myself until the age of forty-six (twenty years after rededicating my life to the Lord), and greatly influenced my decision-making. For example, at the age of twenty, after walking with the Lord for two years, I chose to walk away from Him and for six years of living a rebellious lifestyle, much damage took place within me. During that time, I felt something drop on the inside of me.

After receiving Jesus Christ back into my life, in ***My Story – Part Two***, I share how after many years of seeking the Lord by reading His Word and given to much prayer and fasting, He revealed to me that I had a deep-seated root of rebellion. He also, through a dream, revealed to me what had dropped on the inside of me years earlier, a protective covering, originating from that deep-seated root of rebellion, and how He chose to remove it. This protective covering, fueled by the ingrained carnal core beliefs and mindsets about myself and others, had a negative impact on my feelings, emotions, and behavior. Anger controlled me rather than me having control of anger. Ill feelings, frustrations, and fears would surface when things did not work out my way – especially when my husband, Don, did not act or respond in the way that I thought he should. I was <u>governed</u> by this protective covering and my unregenerate thoughts and feelings and at my core I was very insecure (i.e., low self-esteem, a lack of self-worth or value). I wanted to live out of the new creation, but I could not see how to make that happen (Proverbs 23:7; 1 Peter 1:23; James 1:21; Romans 7:14-25). The incorruptible seed was hidden within my heart and I knew God was with me, but I was not a fruit-bearing Christian and it was very evident in my home (love, joy, peace, longsuffering, gentleness, goodness, faith, meekness, and temperance: against such there is no law – Galatians 5:22-23).

In my mid-forties, after walking with the Lord for twenty years, He directed me to begin to skillfully speak aloud the Words of truth that are now contained in the **Personalized Scripture Guide**, Chapter 4 (Psalm 15:2, 45:1). As the *spirit of my mind* or *inmost mind* was being renewed to the truth of God's Word concerning the born-again creation, it began removing the carnal core beliefs and mindsets that had become strongholds in my life. A picture of the new man began to form within me and by the power of His Holy Spirit, the protective covering was removed. Hallelujah! Through all of this, the new birth became a reality; filling my deepest needs through the wellspring of His living water (John 7:38-39) and I became more Christlike in character, producing the fruit of the Spirit – Galatians 5:22-23. The Lord's intent was to remove those impurities, as dross is removed from precious metals, in order for His image to be seen more clearly within me (Psalm 66:10; Proverbs 25:4). This is His intent for every born-again believer!

Character Development in Christ, is the answer to a prayer I prayed over seventeen years ago. As soon as the protective covering was removed, I felt an opening up within myself and a true connection with the Lord, a wellspring of life (John 7:38). I immediately gasped and said, "This is it! This is what everybody is looking for! How can I help others get here?" Now, over seventeen years later, I am pleased to introduce to you **Character Development in Christ**. In my thirty-seven years of walking with the Lord, the one thing I have struggled with most in my life's quest to know Him and to walk in His ways is my own self-centeredness and the cares of this life. The Bible, in the AMPCE Version, calls the cares of this life "thorn plants." I have concluded as long as I am in this earthen vessel I must surrender these to the Lord, as a gardener removes weeds from his garden (Mark 4:1-20 – AMPCE). Paul said in 1 Corinthians 15:31, *"...I die daily."* Jesus said in Luke 9:23 (NKJV), *"If anyone desires to come after Me, let him deny himself, and <u>take up his cross daily, and follow Me</u>."* The Lord continues to work His righteousness in us; as we go from faith to faith and from glory to glory (Romans 1:17; 2 Corinthians 3:18).

If the Lord is leading you to apply ***Character Development in Christ*** in your own life, I believe you will begin to see several things take place:

1. You will find it easier to trust Him with your day-to-day life and not feel that you have to defend yourself or protect your position.

2. You will see judgments and other carnal thought patterns begin to surface into your conscious thinking where you will need to take them to the Lord to renounce and turn from them. I would also encourage you to share and confess struggles with a mature Christian that you can be open and honest with. Confessing your faults to another, after having confessed them to the Lord, will help you work through some of these areas in your life as you bring them to the light and receive prayer (see Exhibit D). Confession, forgiveness, and healing prayers with members of the body of Christ helps to bring healing to your heart and soul (James 5:16). If you feel you need additional help, please refer to ***Support and Help***.

3. As you begin to put off the old man and put on the new man in Christ, by renewing the *spirit of your mind*, I believe you will see a greater level of spiritual growth, blessing, and peace in your life (Proverbs 21:21, 22:4).

During this season of spiritual growth, my prayer is that your heavenly Father, through your Lord and Savior Jesus Christ, would reveal His heart of love and truth to you in a deeper and greater way, bringing a renewed hope and faith to you through His power, love, wisdom, and goodness. I trust the Lord's transforming power will bring forth the reality of the nature of Christ within your heart and soul. The Lord is very gracious to those who are humble. He is looking for a people who, when they see their faults, are quick to repent and ask for forgiveness from Him and from others where applicable—truly walking in the fear of the Lord! Let's continue to grow up in Christ (1 Peter 2:2)!

God Bless,

Christy Morgan

"...but he is a Jew, which is one inwardly; and circumcision is that of the heart, in the spirit, and not in the letter; whose praise is not of men, but of God" (Romans 2:28-29).

Chapter 1

UNDERSTANDING ITS IMPORTANCE

To better understand the importance of **Character Development in Christ**, let's take a look at part of a prophecy concerning this new creation in Christ. However, we need to consider this background information leading up to the prophecy. Before John the Baptist was conceived, Zacharias, a priest, was in the temple burning incense. Gabriel, the angel of the Lord, appeared to him and spoke to him about his wife, Elizabeth. Gabriel proclaimed to Zacharias that she was going to bear him a son and gave him the baby's name and details concerning his life. Zacharias doubted what the angel said, so Gabriel told him that he would be unable to speak until his words were fulfilled (Luke 1:5-22).

After Elizabeth delivered the child, and on the eighth day when they came to circumcise him, their neighbors and her cousins called him Zacharias, after the name of his father. However, his mother said, "No, he shall be called John." Then Luke 1:62-64 (NKJV) reads,

> *So they made signs to his father—what he would have him called. And he asked for a writing tablet, and wrote, saying, "His name is John." So they marveled. Immediately his mouth was opened and his tongue loosed, and he spoke, praising God.*

The Prophecy:

In Luke 1:67, Zacharias was filled with the Holy Spirit, and prophesied saying,

> *…to perform the mercy promised to our fathers and to remember His holy covenant, the oath which He swore to our father Abraham: <u>to grant us that we, being delivered from the hand of our enemies, might serve Him without fear, in holiness and righteousness before Him all the days of our life</u>.*
> (Luke 1:72-75, NKJV)

(Please note that all who are Christ's are Abraham's seed and heirs according to the promise – Galatians 3:27-29.)

Zacharias clearly prophesied that righteousness and holiness is the divine essence of the born-again creation! Paul tells us to yield our members as servants to righteousness unto holiness (Romans 6:19). As we choose to put on Christ, we are putting on His righteousness, which results in holiness (purification or sanctification), a product of the Holy Spirit. This righteousness cannot come from our human nature for Isaiah 64:6 reads, *"…and all our righteousnesses are as filthy rags…"* Isaiah 32:17 (AMPCE) tells us what His righteousness produces, *"And the effect of righteousness will be peace [internal and external], and the result of righteousness will be quietness and confident trust forever."*

In 1 Peter 3:4, Peter is exhorting married women to live out of the hidden man of the heart (the born-again creation within) as it relates to submitting to their husbands, so that even if they do not obey the Word of God, they may be won over by the behavior of their wives. *"But let it be the hidden man of the heart, in that which is not corruptible –* (as it is produced by an incorruptible seed – 1 Peter 1:23) *– even the ornament of a meek (gentle) and quiet spirit, which is in the sight of God of great price."* Living out of the hidden man of the heart, a gentle and quiet spirit, is a product of the peace of God springing forth from the born-again creation whose confident trust is in Christ. God has called us to crucify the old man—our carnal nature, which keeps us bound to the law of sin and death and to put on the new man—His divine nature, that lifts us up and out of our sinful nature to abundant life in Christ (Romans 8:1-6).

Paul provides us with the key on how to put on and how to operate out of this divine nature.

> *But ye have not so learned Christ; if so be that ye have heard him, and have been taught by him, as the truth is in Jesus: that ye put off concerning the former conversation (behavior) the old man, which is corrupt according to the deceitful lusts; and be renewed in the spirit of your mind; and that ye put on the new man, which after God is created in righteousness and true holiness.*
>
> (Ephesians 4:20-24)

Only through this renewal process can we truly put on the new man.

The word "renewed" in the Greek is *ananeoo*, meaning "to renovate, i.e. reform:– renew." The word "spirit" in the Greek is *pneuma*. The definition in the Thayer's Greek Lexicon when referring to the *spirit of your mind* is "the governing spirit of the mind." After several years of studying and meditating on this particular passage of Scripture, I believe the *spirit of your mind* to be the life source, the power source, and the energy source of the mind—giving life, power, and energy to our beliefs—causing our thought patterns relating to those beliefs to operate automatically without having to consciously think about them. Simply put, it can be identified as the part of us where automatic programs are continually running in order for us not to have to consciously think about everything that we do or say (e.g., our beliefs—what we believe to be true about ourselves). It plays a major role in shaping our behavior and character, our habits, and things we have learned, such as driving a car or riding a bike. Psychologists call this our subconscious.

The Lord confirmed this to me by giving me a revelation concerning the word *reins* in the Bible. Let's look at the following passages of Scripture:

- Psalm 26:2 – *David said, "Examine me, O LORD, and prove me; try my reins and my heart."*
- Jeremiah 17:10 – *I the LORD search the heart, I try the reins, even to give every man according to his ways, and according to the fruit of his doings.*
- Revelation 2:23 – *Jesus said, "... and all the churches shall know that I am he which searcheth the reins and hearts: and I will give unto every one of you according to your works."*

The word "reins" in Hebrew is *kilyah,* which means "a kidney (as an essential organ); figuratively, the mind (as the interior self):–kidneys, reins." The word "reins" in Greek is *nephros* which means "a kidney (plural), i.e. (figuratively) the inmost mind:–reins." In looking up the synonyms for "*inmost mind*," two words stuck out to me—subconscious and spirit. This, I believe, is what Paul is referring to in Ephesians 4:23, "be renewed in the *spirit of your mind* or your *inmost mind*." One correlation between the kidneys and the *inmost mind* is that the kidneys are located deep within the body and the *inmost mind* is located deep within the soul (I'll share more about this later in this chapter, page 10, and in **My Story – Part Two**, page 44).

The following passages describe the innermost part of man:

- Proverbs 18:8, 26:22 – *The words of a talebearer are as wounds, and they go down into the innermost parts of the belly.*

- Proverbs 20:27, 30 – *The spirit of man is the candle of the LORD, searching all the inward parts of the belly. The blueness of a wound cleanseth away evil: so do stripes the inward parts of the belly.*
- Proverbs 24:3-4 – *Through wisdom is an house builded; and by understanding it is established: And by knowledge shall the chambers (innermost part) be filled with all precious and pleasant riches.*

The Hebrew word for "innermost," "inward parts," and "chambers" is the word *cheder* meaning "an apartment…" When referring to Romans 12:2 – *"And be not conformed to this world: but be ye transformed by the renewing of your mind…,"* Missler describes in detail the correlation between the Old Testament temple that Solomon built which housed the Ark of the Covenant in the Holy of Holies and our temple where God lives. Missler shares about the Hebrew word *chedar* to describe our subconscious, as there is no mention of the word subconscious in the Bible. In describing these secret chambers, "One definition for these secret chambers might be: *a hidden reservoir of mostly untrue beliefs and assumptions, which strongly influence how we evaluate all that happens to us in the present and upon which we make our choices. These choices then determine our actions* (p. 216)."[1] We must not underestimate the power of the mind as it relates to our belief system! I believe, as born-again believers, there are ungodly beliefs rooted in pride, selfishness, and fear identifying us contrary to the will and purpose of God that move us to act out in ungodly ways without consciously thinking about it. Paul explains in Romans 7:14-8:6 and Galatians 5:16-26, ungodly beliefs fuel the carnal nature in the same way that godly beliefs fuel the divine nature. So, how does this work?

First, let's look at the word *renewed* a little closer by reading Colossians 3:10, *"And have put on the new man, which is renewed in knowledge after the image of him that created him."* The word "renewed" here in the Greek is <u>anakainoo</u>, which also means "to renovate:–renew." In the Thayer's Greek Lexicon, one meaning for the root word *ana* denotes "<u>repetition</u>, renewal." The Greek word for "renewing" in Romans 12:2 is <u>anakainosis</u>. Its meaning in the Thayer's Greek Lexicon is "a renewal, renovation, complete change for the better." Being renewed in knowledge causes a change to take place on the inside of us (2 Corinthians 3:18, 4:6-7). It's the same thing that occurs when a caterpillar changes into a butterfly, a process called metamorphosis. Let's look, again, at Romans 12:2 (NKJV) which clearly reveals this very fact, *"And do not be conformed to this world, but be transformed by the renewing of your mind, that you may prove what is that good and acceptable and perfect will of God."* In this passage of Scripture, the word "transformed" in the Greek is *metamorphoo*, which means "to transform (literally or figuratively, "metamorphose"):–change, transfigure, transform."

As you can see, in Romans 12:2, Ephesians 4:23, and Colossians 3:10 the word renewed has to do with the mind. This is where the renovation must take place in order for the Lord to bring true transformation within us. What needs to be renovated or removed and replaced with the truth of God's Word are the ingrained carnal core beliefs and mindsets, including vows and judgments, that formed throughout our lives, especially during our formative years concerning ourselves and others. The word "ingrained" means "1. (of a habit, belief, or attitude) firmly fixed or established; difficult to change. 2. (of dirt or a stain) deeply embedded and thus difficult to remove."[2] When looking at the meaning of ingrained let's look at the following passage of Scripture:

> *Husbands, love your wives, even as Christ also loved the church, and gave himself for it; that he might sanctify and cleanse it with the washing of water by the word, that he might present it to himself a glorious church, not having spot, or wrinkle, or any such thing; but that it should be holy and without blemish.*
>
> (Ephesians 5:25-27)

The word "spot" in the Greek is *spilos* meaning "a stain or blemish." It is the root word for *spiloo* meaning "to stain or soil (literally or figuratively):–defile, spot." This word is mentioned only twice in the New Testament, James 3:6 and Jude 1:23. Let's look at James 3:6,

> *And the tongue is a fire, a world of iniquity: so is the tongue among our members, that it defileth the whole body, and setteth on fire the course of nature; and it is set on fire of hell.*

The word "defileth" in the Greek is *spiloo*. This is very important! Just as a stain becomes ingrained in wood or clothing, so too core beliefs become ingrained within us. The Lord's desire is to sanctify and cleanse us from all defilement or ingrained carnal core beliefs and mindsets through the power, purity, and life flow of His Word. You will see examples of this in ***My Story – Part One***, and in ***Part Two*** where I share how those core beliefs were still active even after walking with the Lord for many years.

Now, let's take a look at a couple of examples in my own life in order to help explain how the *spirit of your mind* or your *inmost mind* works. As a little girl learning how to ride my bike, it took many conscious tries learning how to balance on two wheels and at times becoming very frustrated. One night I had a dream, and in the dream, I saw myself riding my bike. When I awoke the next morning, I felt empowered and confident that I could ride that bike before I ever got on it! As soon as I got myself ready, I went outside and got on my bike and I started riding it! I could then talk and laugh with my friends when we would go bike riding, no longer having to consciously think about it. It had become automatic. Another example is when I was learning how to drive a car. I had to consciously think about what I was doing, especially because my dad was teaching me how to drive a car with a manual transmission. He <u>repetitively</u> and <u>patiently</u> worked with me and then one day, I got it! I could listen to the radio and think about other things while I was driving. It had become automatic.

Renewing the *spirit of your mind* or your *inmost mind* to the new man, the born-again creation within, is based on the same principle. This process has no definitive time frame. It takes as long as it takes for the <u>repetitive</u> process of speaking aloud personalized Scriptures "<u>and receiving them as your own</u>," for the power, purity, and life of His Word to become a consistent flow into your *inmost mind*. As a reminder, earlier in this chapter, I shared that the word "reins" in both the Hebrew and Greek means, "kidney, (figuratively) mind or inmost mind." Therefore, as the kidneys remove toxic waste from the blood to keep the body healthy, in the same way, the *inmost mind*, as the life of His Word becomes a consistent flow, filters and flushes out ingrained carnal core beliefs and mindsets or toxic waste (e.g., rebellion, pride, insecurities, rejection), the primary source of the old man (Leviticus 17:11; John 6:63; Ephesians 5:25-27; 1 Peter 1:22-2:3, 3:1-4). As you do this, I believe you will begin to see real change take place in your life (Joshua 1:8).

Here are some additional Scripture references concerning this subject matter: Psalm 1:1-3, 15:1-2, 37:30-31, 40:8 (the perfect law of liberty – Romans 13:10, 13-14 and James 1:18-26), Psalm 51:6, 119:11, 97; Proverbs 18:20-21; Isaiah 26:3; Mark 4:1-20; Luke 6:45-49; Acts 20:32; Romans 6:18-23, 7:22-8:10; 1 Corinthians 2:16 (Colossians 1:26-27); 2 Corinthians 3:3, 18, 5:17, 7:1; Galatians 3:27-29, 5:19-26, 6:15-16; Ephesians 5:8-10; Colossians 2:6-7,11-12; 2 Timothy 2:22; Titus 2:11-14; Hebrews 4:12-13, 5:13-14, 12:14; James 3:1-18; 1 Peter 1:22-2:3; 2 Peter 1:1-10, 16-21; 1 John 2:28-29, 3:7-10.

Because of the work the Lord has done in my own heart and mind through speaking aloud the Scriptures contained in the ***Personalized Scripture Guide***, I am also convinced that He uses the tongue to skillfully write His Words upon the heart, by His Spirit.

- Psalm 45:1 – *...my tongue is the pen of a ready writer.* The word "ready" in Hebrew is *mahiyr* meaning "quick; hence, skillful: diligent, hasty, ready."
- Proverbs 7:1-3 (NKJV) – *My son, keep my words, and treasure my commands within you. Keep my commands and live, and my law as the apple of your eye. Bind them on your fingers; write them on the tablet of your heart.*
- 2 Corinthians 3:2-3 (NKJV) – *...clearly you are an epistle of Christ, ministered by us, written not with ink but by the Spirit of the living God, not on tablets of stone but on tablets of flesh, that is, of the heart.*

Another passage of Scripture that relates to this subject matter is found in 1 Peter 1:13-16, which reads:

> *Therefore gird up the loins of your mind, be sober, and rest your hope fully upon the grace that is to be brought to you at the revelation of Jesus Christ; as obedient children, not conforming yourselves to the former lusts, as in your ignorance; but as He who called you is holy, you also be holy in all your conduct, because it is written, "Be holy, for I am holy."*
> (1 Peter 1:13-16, NKJV)

The Greek word for "gird" is *anazonnymi*, which means "to gird afresh:–gird up" and has the same root word *ana* (repetition). In the Thayer's Greek Lexicon the word "gird" is described as "a metaphor derived from the practice of the Orientals, who in order to be unimpeded in their movements were accustomed, when about to start on a journey or engage in any work, to bind their long flowing garments closely around their bodies and fasten them with a leathern girdle." The Greek word for "loins" is *osphys* meaning "procreative power." As born-again believers, we have a spiritual race to run and it is important for us to renew the *spirit of our minds* or the power source of our minds to the new man in Christ in order to remove any dangling areas of our unregenerate thought patterns! As we choose to do this, Hebrews 4:12 (NKJV) clearly reveals that the Word of God produces results –

> *For the word of God is living and powerful, and sharper than any two-edged sword, piercing even to the division of soul and spirit, and of joints and marrow, and is a discerner of the thoughts and intents of the heart.*

It is essential for us to make conscious efforts to renew the *spirit of our minds* to the born-again creation within as Proverbs 23:7 (NKJV) reads, *"For as he thinks in his heart, so is he..."* In Hebrew the word "thinks" is *shaar*, meaning "to split open or, i.e... to act as a gatekeeper; (figuratively) to estimate:–think." The word "heart" is *nephesh*, which means "a breathing creature, soul." This Hebrew word is used over 450 times in the Old Testament when referring to the soul of man. <u>So, whatever we choose to consistently open ourselves up to, we will become</u>. An example of this is found in **My Story. Part One** mentions that I was born female but I saw myself on the inside as male at the young age of six and lived out of that false identity for twenty years. In giving myself over to that belief and the feelings and thoughts associated with it, I became a homosexual and truly believed I was born that way. In **Part Two**, I continued to surrender my life to the Lordship of Jesus Christ, receiving healing from my deepest wounds, deliverance from my greatest fears, and renewing the *spirit of my mind* or my *inmost mind* to the truth of God's Word concerning the new man in Christ. Through this healing and renewal process, the wholeness and completeness that I had been searching for in a woman was fulfilled through His transforming power (Colossians 2:10).

Colossians 3 and Ephesians 4 and 5 are the foundational chapters used for **Character Development in Christ**. In these chapters, Paul admonishes us to put off the old man and to put on the new man through the renewal process, describing the outward manifestations of both and declaring,

> *For you were once darkness, but now you are light in the Lord. Walk as children of light (for the fruit of the Spirit is in all goodness, righteousness and truth), finding out what is acceptable to the Lord.*
> (Ephesians 5:8-10, NKJV)

The old man comes from our first birth, independent from God and rooted in pride, selfishness, and fear (Psalm 51:5; John 3:1-6; Romans 5:12, 14, 17; 1 Corinthians 15:21-22). This old man represents the foreskin of our hearts and must be removed in order for us to walk in newness of life (Deuteronomy 10:16; Jeremiah 4:4; Colossians 2:11-15). The Lord who is the Word of God, in cooperation with our will, circumcises or removes the old man with its protective coverings (John 1:1, 14; Revelation 19:11-13; Colossians 2:10-11; Hebrews 4:12).

Paul said in Philippians 3:3, *"For we are the circumcision, which worship God in the spirit, and rejoice in Christ Jesus, and have no confidence in the flesh."* He also said in

Colossians 2:11-12 (NKJV) – *"In Him you were also circumcised with the circumcision made without hands, by putting off the body of the sins of the flesh, by the circumcision of Christ…"* Jesus said in John 4:24 – *"God is a Spirit: and they that worship him must worship him in spirit and in truth."* This is why the law, given by Moses, could not make us perfect or complete in character; it would take a total transformation through the death, burial, and resurrection of our Lord and Savior, Jesus Christ (Hebrews 8:5-13, 10:1-10). Again, Paul said in Romans 12:2 (NKJV) – *"And do not be conformed to this world, but be transformed by the renewing of your mind, that you may prove what is that good and acceptable and perfect will of God."* As born-again believers, this transformation begins in the inner recesses of our hearts where His Holy Spirit resides; and continues as we choose to renew the *spirit of our minds* and put on the new man. Jesus said,

> *He that believeth on me, as the scripture hath said, <u>out of his belly shall flow rivers of living water</u> (but this spake he of the Spirit, which they that believe on him should receive: for the Holy Ghost had not been given; because that Jesus was not yet glorified).*
>
> (John 7:38-39)

The word "belly" in the Greek is *koilia*, which means "a cavity, i.e. (especially) the abdomen; by implication, the matrix; figuratively, <u>the heart:–belly, womb</u>." This meaning is different from the meaning where the word heart is mentioned over 150 times in the New Testament; for example, where Peter said in 1 Peter 3:4, *"…let it be the hidden man of the heart."* The word "heart" here in the Greek is *kardia*, which means "the heart, i.e. (figuratively) the thoughts or feelings (mind); also (by analogy) the middle:–(+ broken) heart(-ed)." The Thayer's Greek Lexicon, when referring to "heart" in this passage of Scripture is "the center and seat of spiritual life, the soul or mind, as it is the fountain and seat of the thoughts, passions, desires, appetites, affections, purposes, endeavors (so in English heart, inner man, etc.)." The heart is located in the core of your being where life is conceived and where your true essence is formed. This is where the hidden man of the heart resides and requires spiritual nourishment and strength in order to grow and to mature, and this is obtained through the power, purity, and life flow of God's Word (Psalm 12:6, 119:9; John 6:63; Hebrews 4:12; 1 Peter 1:23-2:3, 3:4).

Peter said in 1 Peter 1:23, *"Being born again, not of corruptible seed, but of incorruptible, by the word of God, which liveth and abideth for ever."* In this incorruptible seed is the very character and nature of God. As born-again believers, our destiny is to be conformed to the image of Jesus Christ (Romans 8:29). It's the same process that takes place with any seed in the natural, as every seed has a destiny to produce after its own kind (Genesis 1:11-12, 21-22, 24-28 – e.g., mankind, plant life, fish, birds, animals). Let's take an apple seed for example; a fruit-bearing apple tree is in the DNA of every apple seed and when planted in good ground, with plenty of water and sunlight, what is hidden within the seed begins to grow into its destiny—a fruit-bearing apple tree.

You can apply that same principle to how we become Christlike; growing into strong men and women of faith and character. First, we must be born again by an incorruptible seed, the Word of God, through (1) repentance - repent and be baptized in the name of the Lord Jesus Christ for the remission of sins, and receive the gift of the Holy Spirit (Mark 1:15, 6:12; John 3:1-6; Acts 2:38; 1 Peter 1:2-2:3), (2) confessing Jesus Christ as Lord—believe on the Lord Jesus Christ. Give oneself to and put one's confidence and trust in Him (John 20:31; Acts 16:31, 19:4; Romans 10:8-13). Then, in order for this incorruptible seed to grow in strength and maturity, Scripture states that His Word is likened to water, light, and nourishment (Ephesians 5:26; Titus 3:5; Psalm 119:130; John 6:35, 51; 1 Corinthians 3:1-3). Through the renewal or transformation process, the incorruptible seed within begins to grow into its destiny, which is to be conformed to His image, *"Christ in you, the hope of glory"* (1 Peter 1:22-2:3; Ephesians 4:20-24; Romans 12:1-2, 8:29; Titus 3:5; Galatians 2:20-21; 2 Corinthians 3:18; Colossians 1:27).

As we submit to the Lordship of Jesus Christ, in obedience to His will, the Lord is faithful to remove the old man with its protective coverings, healing our deepest wounds (Proverbs 18:8, 20-21, 20:27, 30; 1 Peter 2:24 – by His stripes we are healed), delivering us from our greatest fears, and bringing forth the new man. The very character and nature of God growing from the inner recesses of our hearts—this is God's grace! It is written,

> *So now, brethren, I commend you to God and to the <u>word of His grace</u>, which is able to build you up and give you an inheritance among all those who are sanctified.*
>
> (Acts 20:32, NKJV)

In order for this to happen, it requires more than just going to church once or twice a week, saying a prayer over our food three times a day, and a prayer at bedtime. These things are all good and have benefits; but in order to walk in newness of life we must surrender our lives to the Lordship of Jesus Christ and cooperate with the Lord by renewing our minds to His truths in order to put on the new man.

Chapter 2

MY STORY
Part One

In this section I share specific examples of core beliefs that were formed during my childhood. In doing so, I believe you will see how powerful the soul is, and in particular the *inmost mind*, in forming and reinforcing our identity and character during our formative years. I internalized certain events. In particular, one main event influenced the way I saw myself and played a major role in who I became at the age of puberty and into my young adult life. In **My Story – Part Two**, in my early forties, after being born again for thirteen years and married for ten years, I share how the Lord revealed to me that these beliefs were still operating within me, acting as an invisible force or undercurrent and negatively influencing my feelings, emotions, and behavior. These beliefs were not in agreement with the character and nature of the born-again creation and were holding me captive to the old man, robbing me of my true identity and inheritance in Christ. I am thankful that I can also share with you how He led me to dismantle them. I am hopeful that as you read through **My Story – Part One and Two** you will continue to clearly see the importance of renewing the *spirit of your mind* or your *inmost mind* to the new man in order to walk in newness of life. It is only through Christ that we can be healed and set free from our past hurts, fears, and carnal core beliefs and mindsets in order to walk in His abundant life.

Growing up, as far back as I can remember, I was a tomboy (See Exhibit A). I enjoyed pretending to be a cowboy, playing with toy army men, climbing trees, going fishing with my dad, playing softball, and wanting to be the boy when all of the girls in the neighborhood played house. The only time I would even consider playing with dolls is when my sister and I played with Barbie dolls. She would be Barbie and I would be Ken. This behavior seemed very normal to me and very innocent in my thinking. My childhood consisted of parents who loved my sister and me and were not abusive in any way. I have many good childhood memories, and I thank the Lord for my parents who have always been good to both of us. The extent of my Christian upbringing was very shallow, consisting of going to church maybe two or three times a year and being water baptized. There were certain periods throughout my childhood when we would attend Sunday morning services more frequently, but we were not "raised in church."

Between 1997-2000, when I was in my early forties, and after twelve years of marriage, the Lord had my husband Don and me in a season of inner healing. During that time, He had us separately involved in Christian counseling for eight months and then a program called *Living Waters*. While going through counseling, the Lord showed me something that happened during my childhood that had a major impact on what I believed to be the truth about myself.

One December night in 1997, after attending four counseling sessions, He gave me a dream. In the dream, I was standing outside in a wilderness-type area holding something in my hand. It seemed to be made of a hard clay-type substance and was hollow inside. In my other hand I had an instrument, like a dull knife, scraping around the outside of the hollow area, taking the edges off. While doing this, I realized that there might be something in there that I had stirred up, so I dropped the object on the ground. When I dropped it, three bees came out of it and I began to run from them. They were right behind me and were at least seven times larger than a normal bee. As I was running, the only place of safety that I could see was a large building very close in proximity. When I got to the building, I pulled open the door—relieved that it was open. As I ran in, one bee came in with me.

In the building, there were many rooms. I saw a couple of people in one room and tried to get to that room but couldn't. I ran to another room that was vacant and shut the door behind me. With my hands on the door, pressing against it to keep the bee from coming in, I found that the bee's strength was greater than mine. It began pushing the door open. The fear that it was going to hurt me was overwhelming! When it forced its way in, it was a healthy-looking little boy. He had dark hair and bee wings on his back. When I saw that it was a little boy instead of a bee, a feeling of relief came over me. He looked at me as he walked past me and headed toward a toy box that was against the wall. He started looking in it and pulling out toys. As he was preoccupied with the toys in the toy box, I went into another room to try to get away from him; but he followed me into the other room, and that was the end of the dream.

The next morning, I wrote the dream down and took it to my next counseling session. I shared it with my two counselors and both were confident that the dream was from the Lord. Based on their counsel, I released the little boy to Jesus and they prayed over me concerning the situation. They also assured me that the Lord would be faithful to reveal to me the interpretation of the dream. It was not until years later that I began to earnestly inquire of Him the meaning of the dream and it was then that He gave me the interpretation:

> In the dream, I was in a wilderness area, not much going on in my life. I was a stay-at-home mom and housewife with a three-year-old son and a one-year-old daughter. I found myself in the same role as my mother. My life seemed rather dull and boring and my tasks seemed menial. Within myself, I was in a miserable place! The hard clay substance that I was holding in my hand was my heart. The hollowness within it represented how I saw myself as not having much worth or value. The dull knife I was using to scrape around the outside of the hollow area, taking the edges off, was my submission to the Lord's will to the best of my ability. While doing this, I was fearful as I realized that there were some serious problems within me and I knew I needed help.
>
> The bees that came out of the hard clay substance represented fear and hurtful behavior, which at the time was playing a major role in my life. The building in the dream represented a place of refuge (i.e., members of the body of Christ whom the Lord works through to help bring inner healing to His people). When I made haste to run into that place of safety, one bee came in with me. The Lord chose to bring to light something that was operating in my heart in order to set me free. It involved a particular event that had taken place in my early childhood that had produced within me a great amount of fear. The room represented my heart, and the toy box represented the maturity level in my life when this incident took place. The bee wings on the little boy's back represented the strength of fear that gave him access into my heart. Through the dream, the Lord helped me to see that this little boy had been with me for a very long time. The other room that I went into represented a transition when I received Jesus back into my life and no longer desired to identify with that little boy, but he was still with me.

When I was about five or six years old, my mom, my sister, and I were in our car on the way home from running errands. I was sitting in the back seat directly behind my mom. My sister, who is four years older than me, was sitting in the front seat. Mom was driving slowly, as we were in a neighborhood area, and she mistakenly went through a 4-way stop. There was a lady who was already stopped at the 4-way, and when Mom went through it, the lady began to follow us. Mom was a little concerned, so she pulled over right before we got to our house, as she did not want her to see where we lived. The lady passed us and turned around in the next driveway. She drove up to our car and stopped. They both rolled down their windows, and the two of them began yelling and screaming at each other. At that moment, I was overwhelmed with fear and I said within myself, "I <u>can't</u> be like her (my mom)!" The Lord helped me to see that the fear that took place within me that day, subconsciously caused me to be afraid to grow up, and through the strength of that fear, gave way to the little boy causing me to live out of a false identity for many years to come. Nothing was ever mentioned by my mom, my sister, or me about what took place that afternoon. Soon after the Lord revealed this to me, I reminded my sister about that event and how devastated I felt as a young child. I asked her if she remembered the incident, and, if so, was she influenced by it at all. She said she did remember it, but she did not internalize it the way I did. Maybe because she was four years older and could process things in a more mature way, or maybe because we all process things differently. What may seem traumatic to one sibling may not have an impact at all on the other.

Also, while going through Christian counseling and the *Living Waters Program*, the Lord revealed to me more core beliefs about myself and others that formed during my childhood. I combined the two most powerful beliefs about myself into one, as I believe they go hand in hand. The other three were very subtle, as they were not associated with any type of trauma or overwhelming fear, but had a major impact on the way I saw myself and my perception of truth. These beliefs became true and concrete as I internalized behavior patterns from significant others, as well as thoughts generated within myself. These beliefs about myself and others contributed to numerous problems in my life and marriage:

1. <u>*I can't be like her (my mom)! I feel awkward, I feel like a reject!*</u> I believe the Lord helped me to see that the incident that I'm about to share with you is a direct result of what had taken place earlier concerning my mother. There is another factor that I share in **Part Two** that I believe contributed to this as well. At the age of six, my mom had scheduled my sister and me to have a professional portrait made (see Exhibit B). She had fixed my hair and picked out a pretty dress for me to wear. As I looked in the mirror to see what I looked like, what I saw in the mirror did not reflect how I saw myself on the inside. <u>The mirror reflected a little girl, but inside I saw myself as, and felt like, a little boy.</u> Feeling

comfortable on the inside as a boy and feeling awkward at the fact that I was born female, I thought perhaps a mistake had been made and that I should have been born a boy. I was too ashamed to tell anyone about how I was feeling because I felt there was something wrong with me; throughout my childhood years and early adult life, I longed to be a boy as I believed that would have brought normalcy to me and my life would have been so much more enjoyable.

One thing fueling this belief is that I did not feel I had the substance or what it took to be a female, as my character and natural tendencies did not reflect the way femininity was portrayed to me (e.g., by my mother, my sister, my peers, television). I believe there were two factors that greatly contributed to my deep need for a woman's love and touch at a very young age:

- The interpretation of the dream that I shared earlier, how my maturity level became stuck as a child (the little boy in the dream).

- I needed more of my mother's nurturing heart than she had the grace or the ability to give to me (details in **Part Two**, page 39).

Did my dad play a part in any of this? Absolutely! First, I want to express my love, appreciation, and respect for him. Throughout my childhood, he was consistent in his love and faithfulness to my mom, my sister, and to me. He was a hard worker and a good provider, and I am thankful for his commitment to us. However, my dad was a babe in Christ and was ignorant of Satan's craftiness (Ephesians 6:10-12). He did not exhibit the example of what God said his role was as the masculine head of the household. He abdicated that role and gave it to my mom, distorting my perception of what a husband and a father should be according to God's design. This also distorted my view of my heavenly Father, as I saw my dad as distant and unengaged (i.e., a silent partner when it came to raising my sister and me). We both needed from him true masculine strength–teaching, guidance, and instruction–to help us grow in Christ and to help prepare us to face life's challenges. *"And, ye fathers, provoke not your children to wrath: but bring them up in the nurture and admonition of the Lord"* (Ephesians 6:4).

While on this subject, I would like to take a few moments to share about the things I have learned over the years concerning the importance of raising children in the nurture (training) and admonition of the Lord (Genesis 18:17-19; Deuteronomy 6:1-9; Ephesians 6:4). I understand the struggles many Christian parents go through in their quest to raise their children according to God's will. As you will see in **Part Two**, due to my own ingrained carnal core beliefs and mindsets, fears, and insecurities, there were many times my actions and behavior did not display the character and nature of Christ to my husband and children. We all need our Creator's divine nature flowing in and through us, as this is the only way to obtain strength of character in Christ. Children, especially during their formative years, need this impartation from Mom and Dad – *"...Christ in you, the hope of glory"* (Colossians 1:27). Unfortunately, too many of us do not know how to tap into this wellspring of life (John 7:38-39). It was only through the renewal or sanctification process that I began to tap into this reality. This, I believe, was the same dilemma Paul faced in Romans 7. He understood there was a law working in his members keeping him from walking in the fullness of Christ. Jesus died to free us from that law, *the law of sin and death*, through the new birth and the sanctification process, to live out of a new law, *the law of the Spirit of life in Christ Jesus*. The way we do this is to renew our minds to the truth that is in Christ and put on the new man (Ephesians 4:20-24). Paul confirms this as he ends Romans 7 and continues in Romans 8:

> *O wretched man that I am! Who shall deliver me from the body of this death? I thank God through Jesus Christ our Lord. <u>So then with the mind I myself serve the law of God</u>; but with the flesh the law of sin. There is therefore now no condemnation to them which are in Christ Jesus, who walk not after the flesh, but after the Spirit. <u>For the law of the Spirit of life in Christ Jesus hath made me free from the law of sin and death</u>. For what the law could not do, in that it was weak through the flesh, God sending his own Son in the likeness of sinful flesh, and for sin, condemned sin in the flesh: <u>that the righteousness of the law might be fulfilled in us, who walk not after the flesh, but after the Spirit. For they that are after the flesh do mind the things of the flesh; but they that are after the Spirit the things of the Spirit. For to be carnally minded is death; but to be spiritually minded is life and peace</u>.*
>
> (Romans 7:24-8:6)

I believe this is the key to raising children in the nurture (training) and admonition of the Lord, as the reality of the Lord's truth must first be in Mom and

Dad's own heart and mind (Deuteronomy 6:6-8-AMPCE). As we mature in Christ through the renewal or sanctification process, it provides children with a safe and secure environment for healthy mental and emotional development and spiritual growth (Hebrews 4:12-13; Titus 3:3-7; Romans 12:1-2; Ephesians 4:20-24). A child needs the nurture (training) and discipline that comes from parents who have put on Christ (Romans 13:12-14). This helps to enlighten the child to the principles of the Lord's truths, His kingdom rule, and His character and nature, as the child beholds the nature of Christ in Mom and Dad (i.e., tender mercies, kindness, humility, meekness, longsuffering; bearing with one another, and forgiving one another... Colossians 3:12-13 NKJV). For example, through the renewal or sanctification process in my own life, the Lord began to reveal to me the importance of clothing myself with humility (1 Peter 5:5). On one occasion, during a time of fasting and prayer, He spoke to my heart and impressed upon me to initiate a family meeting anytime I acted out of anger toward my children. At that time, Jonathan was five and Jessica was three. He impressed upon me that He wanted me to confess my faults to Jonathan and to Jessica "in front of their daddy," and to tell them that what I did was not right and to ask them to forgive me, and to ask Don to forgive me also (details are provided in ***Part Two***, page 37-38, as well as the revelation the Lord showed me in my obedience). If a child is raised in this type of environment, I believe a spiritual inheritance is deposited within the child's heart and mind to (1) help prepare the child to face life's challenges, and (2) help the child to make the wise choice to flee youthful lusts, and follow after righteousness, faith, love, and peace with those who call on the Lord out of a pure heart (2 Timothy 2:22; Proverbs 22:6).

It is very important to understand that the actions and behavior from both parents, especially the same-sex parent, plays a major role in a child's mental and emotional development and spiritual growth. The same-sex parent acts as a mirror to the child who is growing into his or her image and this is why it is essential for parents to put on Christ (Romans 13:10-14; 2 Corinthians 3:17-18; Galatians 5:22-26; Ephesians 4:20-24; Colossians 3:12-13). The same-sex parent's actions and behavior can either cause a child to embrace who he or she is growing to become based on a sense of security and safety; or reject who he or she is growing to become based on a sense of insecurity and fear. If a child rejects either Mom or Dad's actions and behavior, especially the same-sex parent, it can cause the child to defensively detach and not be able to receive the Lord's intent for healthy mental and emotional development and spiritual growth. This does not necessarily mean that the child will gravitate towards homosexuality; however, a dysfunctional relationship between either parent can result in the child forming inner vows, judgments, bitterness, and/or resentment. If this occurs, these distortions, inner vows and/or bitter root judgments can hold the child captive to the old man or sinful nature. Thank God, Christ came to set us free from the effects of living out of our sinful nature as you will see as I continue with my own life story (Ephesians 2:1-7). For more information on this subject matter, please refer to the ***Scripture Guide Study Notes - Volume 2***, Note 49.

In my young teenage and early adult life, I found myself in homosexual relationships in order to try to meet the deep need that I had for a woman's love and touch at a very young age. As a young child, I respected my mother and saw her as a strong woman and very smart. She always had the final say in our home. However, because she lacked understanding concerning the new birth in Christ and how to walk in that born-again creation, she would become very defensive and hurtful with her words when she felt trespassed against. Even though I loved my mom, and I knew she loved my sister and me, I was afraid of her and was very careful not to cross her in any way. As you will see in ***Part Two***, I was also very defensive and hurtful with my words, especially toward my husband when I felt trespassed against; as I too lacked understanding of the new birth in Christ and how to walk in the born-again creation.

> 2. <u>*I'm stupid, I can't think for myself!*</u> During my formative years, around the age of six, I remember when going to bed in the winter nights it seemed that I was always asking my mom what to cover up with. One winter night when I asked her that question she responded with, "Nothing!" She was getting tired of me always asking her that question and thought that if I got cold enough, I would figure it out for myself. But that wasn't the case, because I thought her word was final, I went the whole night without covering up with anything. Evidently her strategy worked, as I do not recall ever again asking her that question.
>
> Also, when I was about six or seven, after supper one evening while Mom was cleaning up the kitchen, she asked me to take out the trash (back then, we put our trash in brown paper bags that we got from the grocery store). I asked her, "Where do you want me to take it?" She said, "Just go dump it out there on the back porch!" So, I just shrugged my shoulders and went out onto the back porch and dropped it. Everything that was in that bag splattered all over the porch! As I was standing there looking at it, my dad came to the door and asked me what I was doing? I said, "Mom told me to dump this trash out here on the back porch."

Dad seemed a little flustered with it all, but graciously cleaned up the mess. The only thing Mom said was, "I thought you knew where to take the trash!" Even though Mom or Dad never called me stupid, that incident made me feel stupid.

While in elementary and high school, I was afraid to ask my teachers questions because I was fearful that my questions would be perceived as silly or stupid. <u>I truly believed that I was born stupid</u>. As a side note, a year or two after I rededicated my life to the Lord, one day after work, I came home and was lying on my bed with my eyes closed, not really thinking about anything. I saw a vision of a brown paper bag full of trash falling and splattering all over the back porch. I was a little startled, as I had not thought of that incident in many years. As soon as I saw that vision, the Lord spoke to me and said, "There will be times when I will ask you to do things that won't necessarily make sense to you, but I want you to do them." He wanted to assure me that when He tells me to do something that doesn't seem to make sense to me, my obedience will produce fruit.

3. <u>*It's never good enough; there's always something wrong!*</u> When I was eight or nine years old, my mom told me to go take a bath. I decided to do a little extra while taking a bath, thinking she would be proud of me. I always wanted to please her, so I washed myself all over twice. When I told her what I had done, being very excited and proud of myself and thinking that she would be pleased with me too, her response was, "You used the same washcloth to wash yourself twice!?" She didn't approve of how I did the extra, and I said within myself, "<u>It's never good enough!</u>" It was also very difficult for my sister and me to please her when it came to housework. Whatever we did (e.g., making up our beds, dusting), <u>there always seemed to be something wrong</u> with it. When it came to housework, I can only remember one time when she told me she was pleased with what I did.

4. <u>*Females are smarter than males*</u>! Throughout my childhood, I believed that females were smarter than males simply because of the way I saw how my mom and my dad responded to each other. As I mentioned earlier, my mom had the final say in our home; therefore, I thought she was the smarter one. This belief caused lots of problems in my marriage.

These beliefs about myself and others are a product of the carnal nature, internalizing thoughts and feelings apart from the grace and truth of God's Word, as Paul said in Romans 7:18, *"For I know that in me (that is, in my flesh) dwelleth no good thing…"* (References include Genesis 6:5, 8:21). These beliefs about myself produced within me a low self-esteem and a lack of self-worth or value. I was deeply rooted in the fear of man (e.g., their opinions). Deep down I rejected myself and felt that others, after they got to know me, would reject me as well. These beliefs caused a narcissistic stronghold of pride to form within me, which helped hide my profound fears and insecurities. The word stronghold is used only once in the New Testament.

> *For though we walk in the flesh, we do not war after the flesh: <u>(for the weapons of our warfare are not carnal, but mighty through God to the pulling down of strong holds;) casting down imaginations, and every high thing that exalteth itself against the knowledge of God</u>, and bringing into captivity every thought to the obedience of Christ…*
> (2 Corinthians 10:3-6)

"Stronghold" in the Greek is *ochyroma*, meaning "to fortify, through the idea of holding safely); a castle (figuratively, argument):–stronghold." Only God can dismantle strongholds by His Word and through the power of His Holy Spirit. In **Part Two** you will see how the Lord chose to do that for me.

I was thirteen years old when I had my first homosexual relationship. I didn't feel convicted until around the age of fifteen when I wondered if what I was doing was wrong, but I dismissed it. I thought, "How could it be wrong when it feels so right?" During this time, I was drinking alcohol, partaking in other drugs, and "partying" in order to help bring freedom and joy to my bound-up heart! At the age of seventeen, I moved out of my parent's house because I wanted to be free to party and have a good time. I thought I had found what made me happy and brought fulfillment to my life. I was living out of a "foolish/immature heart," as subconsciously, I was afraid to grow up. My maturity level was that of a young child wanting only to party, have fun, and fill the deep longings that I had for a woman's love and tender touch. During this time, I put my parents through much grief and sorrow. I was not open about what I was doing, as I knew it would crush them. I also thought if I told my mom about my lifestyle, she would disown me. I love my parents, who have now gone on to be with the Lord. When I was in my early forties, I shared with them about my past lifestyle and asked them to forgive me for all the grief and sorrow that I had put them through.

At the age of eighteen, my life was interrupted by the Lord's truth. A friend of mine who had come out of the homosexual lifestyle, who was married and walking with the Lord, asked me the following question, "Do you know that homosexuality is wrong?" I responded, "No." (As I stated earlier, there were a couple of times I wondered if it was wrong, but dismissed it.) She handed me a Bible and asked me to read the following passage:

> *Professing themselves to be wise, they became fools, and changed the glory of the uncorruptible God into an image made like to corruptible man, and to birds, and four-footed beasts, and creeping things. Wherefore God also gave them up to uncleanness through the lusts of their own hearts, to dishonor their own bodies between themselves: who changed the truth of God into a lie, and worshipped and served the creature more than the Creator, who is blessed for ever. Amen. <u>For this cause God gave them up unto vile affections: for even their women did change the natural use into that which is against nature: and likewise, also the men, leaving the natural use of the woman, burned in their lust one toward another; men with men working that which is unseemly, and receiving in themselves that recompence of their error which was meet. And even as they did not like to retain God in their knowledge, God gave them over to a reprobate mind, to do those things which are not convenient...</u>*
>
> (Romans 1:22-31)

After I read it, she asked me, "What are you going to do about it?" I responded with, "Well, I guess I'm going to have to quit!"

I began asking questions trying to find answers on how to know the Lord. I remember lying in my bed at night saying, "I love You, Lord; I love You, Lord…" over and over again before going to sleep. I didn't know that I needed to be loved and discipled in the truth by mature Christians. I didn't understand the importance of attending church and having a church family. I also had no clue about being baptized in the Holy Spirit and its importance. I do remember when I would talk to people about the Lord, if they didn't know Him they would easily receive Him into their hearts, and I found myself always talking about Jesus. I knew He was with me. At my apartment, I also had a Bible study once a week which was made up of people who didn't know much about the Lord either. This went on for a while until the age of twenty when I started becoming restless. I was missing my old friends and having fun. At that point, I wasn't thinking about going back into homosexuality, I just wanted to enjoy life. I had no clue that Jesus came to give me life and that more abundantly (John 10:10)! This thought started coming to me, "You're such a pretty young girl, and having Bible studies and talking about the Lord all the time is going to get very boring." This thought was coming from the source of my carnal nature, Satan, in order to pull me off the path I was on (John 14:30; Acts 26:18; Ephesians 2:2, 6:12). Because of my immature heart, it didn't take long for me to begin to act on that thought.

During that time, I was working at AT&T. In the area where I worked, there was a man who was an associate Baptist pastor who I approached with the following question:

> "If there are two people who both know they are saved, one serves the Lord all her life and the other leaves the Lord to go her own way, what would be the difference?"

His answer,

> "They would both go to heaven. The difference would be that the one who served the Lord all of her life would receive rewards, the other would not."

Well, that was all my foolish heart needed to hear, as I did not have an eternal perspective. I was focused only on the temporary (earthly-minded), and therefore, getting old, dying, and going to heaven seemed like eons away. All I cared about was the here and now, and enjoying life. The only thing I cared about concerning spiritual things was making sure that I was going to heaven. I didn't care about receiving rewards, as I couldn't see how you could use them after you were dead anyway! My belief system concerning Christianity was based on works. I thought that I would have to serve Jesus for the rest of my life, no fun or excitement, and then I would go to heaven and see Him. When I realized I could go to heaven without having to serve Him, I felt relieved.

That afternoon on my way home from work I said to the Lord, "<u>I can't serve you and do what I want to do, so I'm going to have to leave</u>." My mind was made up. What a deception! I was twenty years old when I made that decision. The next time I had the Bible study, I told all my friends that I was not going to have it any longer. As they were leaving, I was standing at the front door, and as one girl walked past, she said to me that she was disappointed in my decision because she was starting to believe the Word of God. I can still see the disappointment on her face as if it were yesterday. However, I was so full of pride that I didn't care what anybody thought about my decision. Scripture is very clear in 2 Peter 2:20-22 that it is better for you to have never known the Word of righteousness than to have known it and walked away from it! I didn't understand that I was a new creation on the inside and that God was with me to give me abundant life by having true fellowship with Him. His desire was for this new creation within me to grow up to be like Him on the inside, bearing His image and nature.

One evening, shortly after I made that decision, I went to a gay bar. Later that evening, after having too much to drink and after returning to my apartment, I began to cry as I was crawling up the stairs to my bedroom. I didn't understand then but I understood later, that my born-again spirit, even though still a baby (1 Peter 2:2), was grieving because of the decision I had made. From the age of twenty to the age of twenty-six I went into deep darkness. It didn't happen all at once, little by little my sinful nature became more and more active. I went back into the homosexual lifestyle, along with partying, drinking alcohol, and partaking in other drugs. Ephesians 2:1-5 describes exactly what was going on with me and there was no restraint on my flesh. I conducted myself in the passions of my flesh; my behavior was governed by my corrupt and sensual nature, obeying the impulses and deep cravings of the flesh and thoughts of my mind. I was controlled by the prince of the power of the air, the demon spirit that works in the sons and daughters of disobedience. I was a selfish mess!

During those six years, I came to a place where I didn't even want the Lord's name mentioned to me. On several occasions, random people whom I had never met approached me to share Jesus and I would say, "I don't want to hear it!" There was one guy who tried to share Jesus with me. I literally pushed him away, and told him to be quiet and to leave me alone! Also, during this time, one day I was at my parent's house and my dad and I were outside. I was walking around in their backyard and I felt something drop on the inside of me. I didn't know what it was, but I knew I had gotten something. Shortly after that took place, my self-centeredness along with my hatred and anger (hurtful behavior) began to intensify. I also did not know until later in life that my parents dreaded to see me come over because of my behavior. When I was in my early forties, the Lord gave me a dream that revealed what it was that dropped on the inside of me. He revealed to me the negative impact it had on my life and I share how He chose to remove it. (This is discussed in **Part**

Two, pages 40-43.)

In 1983, at the age of twenty-six, after being in many homosexual relationships and convinced that I was born a homosexual, I had just broken up with someone that I deeply cared for and I was heartbroken. Soon after that relationship ended, I was at a friend's house and everyone had gone to bed. I was alone sitting on the living room floor feeling very empty and hopeless. So much damage had taken place within me as a result of the decision I had made six years prior. I understood later that I had sown so much corruption that the harvest of which I sowed in my life was coming upon me (Galatians 6:7). As I was sitting there, I was trying to think of what path I could take because I could no longer continue on this one. I thought of a couple of paths but they both led to a dead-end street. I had no thoughts of the Lord, nor did I have thoughts of marriage. I had no desire for a husband. I did not understand then, but subconsciously the deeply embedded core belief rooted in fear that, *"I can't be like my mother,"* was still operating within me, keeping me stuck as a young child within myself. I was afraid to grow up. Then this thought came to me, "I wish I could be a little girl again and go back home and live with Mom and Dad." <u>I needed someone greater and stronger than myself to take care of me.</u>

At that moment of humility, I felt the presence of Jesus Christ very close to me. When I looked up toward the ceiling, I saw Him as if He were at a distance, and I knew He had come to save me. I said, "Jesus, please forgive me, I can't make it without you. Please come back into my life." After I had spoken those words, He turned and vanished out of the room. I got up to go to bed and as I walked into the bedroom, I saw a Bible on the nightstand. I felt He was saying to me, "I want you to get to know Me." I picked it up and began reading. I thank the Lord again for His patience and mercy! He looked upon me with a heart of compassion. The Lord knew that the lifestyle I had chosen to live would lead me to a dead-end street, and He had been waiting for years for me to realize that He was the only way to true fulfillment and abundant life. Only He, my Creator, could bring freedom, healing, and maturity to my bound-up and confused heart; I am a living testament of the Lord's power, goodness, and grace!

It wasn't too long after I had asked the Lord to come back into my life that I had the opportunity to receive the baptism of His Holy Spirit. A friend and I were at a conference where Pastor Bob Yandian was ministering the Word of God. At the end of his message, he asked if anyone wanted to receive Jesus Christ as their Lord and Savior. I knew that I had taken care of that. Then he asked, "Is there anyone who would like to receive the baptism of the Holy Spirit?" I felt something rise up within me, so I stood up and at the same time my friend stood up as well. We were then asked to come up front. He said, "From this day forward you will never be the same," and he prayed that the Lord would baptize us with His Spirit (John 1:33; Luke 11:9-13). I became strengthened to do His will and to seek Him (Acts 1:8). I began to pursue the Lord with all of my heart! As hard and persistent as I pursued my former lifestyle, I sought the Lord with that same fervor, and He blessed it! I told the Lord, "I will do anything You want me to do, I will even be a nun if that's what You want; but I do not want to get married."

Also, during this time, one day while at work the reality of feeling like a young child on the inside hit me. At that time, I was a clerical secretary for a district manager and while I was sitting at my desk in my blouse and slacks (as I did not wear dresses until later after I had matured more in the Lord), several men about my age (twenty-six) came to see the district manager. They were all wearing a suit and tie and when I looked up at them, the reality hit me like a ton of bricks; I sensed that they had matured into grown men, and <u>I still felt stuck as a young child on the inside and I didn't know how to change that</u>! The Lord became my strength, and I found peace as I immersed myself in Him.

For three years, from 1983-1986, every waking moment outside of work I was either reading the Bible, praying, going to church, listening to teaching tapes, or serving at the church. I literally immersed myself in His Word, renewing my mind to His truths, and giving myself over to much prayer and fasting. The only thing that I was crying out for was wisdom and understanding. Other than that, I was seeking Him with my whole heart and doing whatever I thought He was asking me to do. He began to exalt me at my workplace, as the Lord's wisdom was with me to do my work with excellence. I had favor with my superiors and within three years I received two promotions, both in management positions. On at least two separate occasions during those three years, I received a Team Award, Exceptional Performance Award, and other bonuses. It was incredible how He was exalting me because of my humbling myself before Him and seeking Him with my whole heart. Glory to the Lord forever!

He also began working in me a desire for a husband and I said to Him, "Lord, You must want me to get married!" I began to pray concerning my future husband, and a few months later the Lord brought him to me. We formally met in June 1986 and were married in September 1986. I knew that I knew through an open vision that the Lord had sent Don to be my husband.

The main thing that Don and I had, and still have in common, is Jesus, as we both love the Lord. This man, too, came out of the homosexual lifestyle. As I share detailed accounts about our marriage in ***Part Two***, I asked Don if he would share his testimony and he graciously said yes. See Chapter 3 for his testimony. Don and I were best friends for the first eight years of our marriage. Seven years after we were married, I became pregnant with our son, Jonathan. After he was born, I became a stay-at-home mom and housewife. When Jonathan was about a year old, our marriage began to unravel. In ***Part Two***, I share how the Lord did a tempering work in me by using my husband and my role as a stay-at-home mom and housewife as an environmental furnace, as the beliefs that had formed during my childhood began to surface. As dross is removed from precious metals, His process of refining my character, or personhood, continued so that His image could be seen more clearly within me (Proverbs 25:4).

MY STORY
Part Two

The strength and maturity that I had gained during the first three years of my walk with the Lord (1983-1986) was undeniable to all who knew me, and I thought His work within me was pretty much complete. However, little did I know that nine years later I would find myself in an environmental furnace. An environment designed by the Lord to remove the ingrained carnal core beliefs that wrongfully identified me, holding me captive to the old man, my carnal nature. Before Don and I met, in May 1986, while attending a Christian International Conference, I received a prophetic word that I would be getting married sooner than soon, and the Lord was going to set us aside to do a tempering work. Don and I formally met in June 1986, and we married three months later. This is what I call "sooner than soon." After being married for nine years to my best friend and one who puts the Lord first place in his life, things began to change as the Lord's tempering work began. During this tempering work, two things became very apparent to me: (1) the depth of my spiritual immaturity, and (2) how powerful *the spirit of the mind*, the *inmost mind,* or the *power source of the mind* is in reinforcing our beliefs, identities, and behavior patterns.

A recap of the core beliefs outlined earlier is important here, as you will recognize them as we continue:

1. *I can't be like her (my mom)! I feel awkward, I feel like a reject!*
2. *I'm stupid, I can't think for myself!*
3. *It's never good enough; there's always something wrong!*
4. *Females are smarter than males!*

This tempering work began in 1995, a year after our son Jonathan was born and a year after I became a stay-at-home mom and housewife. Things were not going too well in the Morgan house, as this was the beginning of a seven-year tempering work. The Lord knew the man that I needed to marry and the environment He needed to put me in where these ingrained carnal core beliefs about myself and my perception of life would begin to surface. These beliefs provided the fuel for my environment to become an environmental furnace. As the heat was being turned up, I could understand why I ran from wanting to be put into this role, as a stay-at-home mom and housewife, in the first place. As I shared earlier, I felt stuck as a young child on the

<u>inside and I didn't know how to change that</u>, and being put into this role intensified those inadequate feelings. I knew much of the Bible, as I had read it over many times, but the reality of the truth of God's Word had not penetrated my heart when it came to the substance of operating and functioning out of the born-again creation, the new man. The fruit of the Spirit was not flowing in me; therefore, I did not have the strength and the wisdom I needed to truly enjoy my God-given tasks as a stay-at-home mom and housewife (Galatians 5:22-23). *(<u>I can't be like her [my mom]! I feel awkward, I feel like a reject</u>!)*

I had gotten my eyes off the Lord and onto Don, who was not meeting my expectations in the areas of sensitivity and decision-making. I saw him as a hard man to live with because of what I perceived as high expectations and control, and I was feeling very angry and resentful about it. During this time, I could better understand and relate to my mother as I thought that I was smarter than Don when it came to having the final say in our home. As a child, I internalized a false belief that the only real value in a husband was to go to work in order to make money to provide for the family, and to leave the rest to the wife. As far as Don was concerned, that was not going to happen! The Lord knew exactly the man that I needed to marry who would touch a deep-seated root of rebellion and hatred within me that I didn't know was there. For example, as I shared earlier, as a child, I thought my mom was very smart in her decision-making, as she had the final say in our home. Therefore, when Don did not make decisions or respond to me in the way that I thought that he should, I could literally feel a "hatred of stupidity" directed toward him. I didn't know what to do about it, but I was very aware that it was there! *(<u>Females are smarter than males</u>!)*

Don was also feeling resentful and bitter toward me as I was not meeting his expectations concerning cleaning house and cooking meals. He resented my behavior patterns when it came to my communication with him and was disappointed that I did not view my role as a stay-at-home mom and housewife as a privilege, joy, and honor. When I was put into this role, I realized that there were things that were operating within me that were not right and I knew I needed help. Because my soul was so entrenched with insecurities (i.e., low self-esteem and a lack of self-worth or value), when Don would share with me his displeasure as to how I cleaned house or cooked a meal, my feelings would get hurt and I would feel threatened, feeling like a child and acting like a child. I would become very defensive and either shut down or lash out in anger. The times when I would shut down, I would brew over the situation and hold a grudge.

I had no clue that this was the Lord's tempering work. I began to understand that even though I loved the Lord, my unregenerate thoughts and feelings derived from the deep-seated beliefs about myself and judgments toward men began to surface when I was put into this role. The word "deep-seated" is defined as "existing for a long time and very difficult to change: firmly established."[1] This opened the door to the enemy of my soul, Satan, to minister half-truths to me concerning my husband and our marriage, as I was convinced that I could not meet Don's expectations. I began to think that I had made a mistake, and that he was not the man that I should have married. I felt like I was in a heated furnace and I wanted out! Furthermore, I did not like him telling me what to do! I remember as a child growing up, I heard my mom say many times, "No man is <u>ever</u> going to tell me what to do!" I felt threatened as I did not feel smart enough or secure enough in my own personage to stand up in the strength and security of the born-again creation, the new man, and also fearful and angry at the fact that I felt more like a child than a wife. *(I can't be like her [my mom]! I feel awkward, I feel like a reject!) (I'm stupid, I can't think for myself!) (It's never good enough; there's always something wrong!)*

When Jonathan was seventeen months old, I was thinking about leaving Don for a few months because I was so miserable. Satan was trying to destroy what God had put together. Let's recall what I said in **Part One**, concerning my husband "...*a few months later the Lord brought him to me. We formally met in June 1986 and were married in September 1986. I knew that I knew through an open vision the Lord had sent Don to be my husband.*" This is an example of how the thief, Satan, comes to steal God's will from our lives (John 10:10). Satan was trying to do the same thing that he did back when I was twenty years old. He was using my carnal thoughts and feelings to try to pull me away from God's will. I give God much thanks for His faithfulness as two weeks later, I found myself pregnant again and that put all the thoughts of leaving on hold. I was married with one child and one on the way, not happy, and blaming my husband for my unhappiness.

One night, I got on my knees and began to repent before the Lord, asking Him to forgive me for not putting Him first in my life. Also, during this time, I had thoughts that the Lord was mad at me and punishing me for walking away from Him at the age of twenty and for all of my past sins and mistakes. However, the Lord revealed to me later that He was pleased with me, and was answering a prayer I had prayed to Him many times, which was and still is, "I want to be like Christ!" His intent was to bring to the surface and remove the ingrained carnal core beliefs and mindsets, as dross is removed from precious metals, in order for His image to be seen more clearly within me. That's why I felt like I was in a heated furnace (Proverbs 25:4)! The Lord's desire was for me to learn how to function and operate out of the born-again creation, the new man. I didn't have a clue as to how that could happen! No matter how sorry I was for my behavior patterns, I needed the Lord to help me see the reality of the life-giving flow of His Words and His Spirit instead of living in a state of defeat and misery.

In March 1996, our daughter Jessica was born. A thick wall was between Don and me, and neither one of us knew how to turn this thing around. In our misery, the Lord began to open doors for us to receive help (i.e., Christian counseling, the *Living Waters Program*). About three months before Jessica was born, the Lord brought a lady by the name of Dee Barnes, the founder of *His Wonderful Works*, into our lives, and to this day she is one of our dearest friends. In the early part of 1997, she shared a brochure with us about a program called *Living Waters*. *Living Waters*, which comes out of Desert Stream Ministries located in Kansas City, Missouri, is a 20-week discipleship and healing program that focuses on sexual and relational wholeness in Christ. At first, Don didn't think this program was for him, as he did not understand the roots of his brokenness, but the Lord graciously helped him to see that it was His will. Don went through the program first, and during that time I began counseling with two Christian ladies. It was during this time that the Lord gave me the dream that I shared in **Part One**. I counseled with these two ladies for eight months, and when dealing with ungodly beliefs, one of the counselors stated:

> "What you truly believe is not what you consciously think is right based on what the Bible says. What you truly believe is what comes out of you when faced with challenging and/or difficult situations."

I didn't understand then, but later I understood this to mean the thought patterns rooted in ingrained carnal beliefs and mindsets that operate on auto-mode through the *spirit of the mind* or the *inmost mind*.

I also shared with them about my relationship with my husband and how miserable we both were. One of the counselors suggested that I begin to journal to the Lord; being real with Him by putting pen to paper or fingers to keyboard, like writing a letter to Him, pouring out my heart and telling Him when circumstances of life or people disrupted my well-being and the feelings associated with it (see Exhibit C for an example of one of my journal entries). She also said there would be times when the Lord would speak to me and to keep a journal of His Words as well. As I began to journal to the Lord, being honest with Him about things in my life (e.g., my fears and insecurities, my faults and shortcomings, my cares and concerns, my anger and frustration), I found some relief from the battle that was going on within me.

David poured his heart out to the Lord in portions of the book of Psalms. In Psalm 142:2 (NKJV) David said, *"I pour out my complaint before Him; I declare before Him my trouble."* David also encouraged others to be open with the Lord. In Psalm 62:8 (NKJV) he said, *"Trust in Him at all times, you people; pour out your heart before Him; God is a refuge for us."* Several times as I was journaling to the Lord, when I would come to the part in my journal entry where the pain, anger, or frustration surfaced, I would become so angry that I would take my pen and jam it through the pages of my notebook, throw my notebook down on the floor, and scream. I would feel bad about my behavior and would ask the Lord to forgive me. Later, He helped me to see, through His Word, that His desire was for Cain to be open and honest with Him in order to help him work through the anger he felt toward his brother, Abel (Genesis 4:6-8). Unfortunately, in Cain's pride, instead of being open and honest with the Lord about his feelings, he chose to take his anger out on his brother and killed him.

The Lord revealed to me that anger can erupt when someone triggers a source of pain or fear (e.g., insecurity) that is associated with a core belief operating within a person's life. I am convinced that the Lord would much rather have us come to Him with our temper tantrums rather than take our frustrations out on others. Only He knows the source of our pain and fears and how to bring healing and freedom to us. He is our Creator, our Father, our Healer, and our Counselor – Genesis 1:26-28; Psalm 139:13-16; Isaiah 9:6; 1 Peter 2:24-25. I share more about this in ***A Personal Prayer Journal – Details and Instructions***, Chapter 5, and in Notes 9 and 27a in the ***Scripture Guide Study Notes - Volume 2***.

Eight months later, after I completed counseling and Don completed the *Living Waters Program*, Don began counseling with the same two ladies and I became a participant in the *Living Waters Program*. In the *Living Waters Program*, each week a different topic was taught concerning our heavenly Father's intent for us, and I began to understand the reality of His love for me at a personal level. The Lord used these teachings to reveal things that had taken place in my life, especially as a young child, where I internalized certain situations and the way I perceived myself and others (e.g., through behavior patterns from significant others as well as thoughts generated from myself or through misconceptions of myself that I had either forgotten or dismissed). These events had a profound impact in forming core beliefs that needed to be removed and replaced with forgiveness, healing, and the truth of God's Word. At the end of each teaching, we would break up into small groups which consisted of 3-5 others of the same sex, a small group leader, and an assistant leader. This provided a safe place to share things the Lord had revealed during the teaching and/or throughout the week (e.g., root issues, shortcomings, weaknesses, hurts, fears, pain). After sharing, we would receive prayer and support where needed.

> *Confess to one another therefore your faults (your slips, your false steps, your offenses, your sins) and pray [also] for one another, that you may be healed and restored [to a spiritual tone of mind and heart]. The earnest (heartfelt, continued) prayer of a righteous man makes tremendous power available [dynamic in its working].*
>
> (James 5:16, AMPCE)

On one occasion during the week, between meeting times, the Lord specifically spoke to my heart and said, "You have a deep-seated root of rebellion." I asked the Lord to forgive me and confessed this to Don. The next time we met I confessed to my small group where I received prayer and encouragement. The Lord has been faithful to remove this from me; however, as *My Story* continues, you will see it took time. I thank God for this ministry! It brought a greater understanding of the Father's heart of love to Don and me. It helped us to see the importance of relationship with the Father and with others, and the importance of honoring and respecting others by taking responsibility for our harmful behavior patterns and walking in humility. As we began to apply these truths in our own personal lives, it helped our marriage to become stronger in the Lord. Christian counseling and *Living Waters* were two very important stepping stones in our walk with the Lord to bring more of the <u>reality</u> of Christ in us as we found freedom in confession with community, helping us to embrace "a new way of living." The healing we received from past hurts and fears through healing prayers from members of the body of Christ, gaining understanding of the importance of confession, and keeping everything in the light with God and others (where applicable) was priceless and became a valuable tool that we continue to use in our quest to know Him and to be more like Him. Because of this, Don and I have volunteered our time as leaders in the *Living Waters Program* since 1998 and we have been able to impart these truths to our children as well.

I began taking responsibility for my outbursts of anger toward my husband by confessing my faults to him and asking for forgiveness even when I didn't feel like it (Ephesians 4:26). I found the times I chose to humble myself in confessing my faults and asking for forgiveness, the more I saw God's grace operating in my life. I began to see that humility was the key that opened the door to His grace. The Lord was teaching me how to clothe myself with humility.

> *...Clothe (apron) yourselves, all of you, with humility [as the garb of a servant, so that its covering cannot possibly be stripped from you, with freedom from pride and arrogance] toward one another. For God sets Himself against the proud (the insolent, the overbearing, the disdainful, the presumptuous, the boastful)–[and He opposes, frustrates, and defeats them], but gives grace (favor, blessing) to the humble.*
>
> (1 Peter 5:5, AMPCE)

However, I wanted to do more than continually apologize. I wanted to live out of the new man in Christ, producing the fruit of the Spirit and living a life of victory (Galatians 5:22-23)! Oh, I had temporary bursts of joy and peace based on my circumstances and how I was feeling at the time, but the life-giving flow of living out of the law of the Spirit of life in Christ Jesus, regardless of circumstances, had not yet become a reality within me (Romans 8:1-6; 2 Corinthians 4:16-18). I was still very much aware of my self-centered nature and how easy it was to enter into my carnal patterns of thinking and feeling when things did not go my way, therefore, becoming very frustrated, angry, and/or discouraged. During times of frustration, usually when I was upset with something Don had said or done, or just because I was ill and didn't want to be bothered, I would lash out in anger toward Jonathan and/or Jessica when they would do the least little thing that aggravated me. I never beat them, but I would raise my voice at them in an angry tone, and I could see how my behavior hurt their feelings. I would feel terrible after I acted out and would ask them to forgive me. Afterwards, I would pour my heart out to the Lord, through journaling, and would ask Him to forgive me as well. On one occasion during a time of fasting and prayer, when Jonathan was five and Jessica was three, the Lord spoke to my heart concerning this issue. He impressed upon me to initiate a family meeting anytime I acted out of anger toward my children. The Lord impressed upon me that He wanted me to confess my faults to Jonathan and to Jessica "in front of their daddy" and to tell them that what I did was not right and to ask them to forgive me and to also ask Don to forgive me. That was very humbling for me, because I didn't want Don to know! I was concerned that he would get upset with me and make me feel even worse than I already felt. However, because of my reverence for the Lord, I did what

He instructed me to do. I knew that even though I was fearful to do it, there would be safety in it, because I was humbling myself by following His instructions. As His Word says in 1 Peter 5:5 and in James 4:6, *"God resists the proud, but gives grace to the humble."*

These family meetings proved to be very rewarding. Don was gracious and blessed my humility and honesty, and after I confessed my faults to Jonathan and Jessica and asked them to forgive me, they would always say, *"You're forgiven Mommy."* During this time, we would ask Jonathan and Jessica if there was anything that was bothering them or hurting them. On several occasions, they would open up their little hearts and share, and where applicable, we would ask them to forgive us. Don also used this time to confess areas of weakness and faults, and at the end of the meeting we would pray. It turned into a very fruitful time for all of us. In the beginning, it seemed I would have to call a family meeting at least once every other week, but as time went on the family meetings grew less and less. I believe in doing this, it helped to remove the hurt, produced by my tongue, from Jonathan and Jessica (James 3:8).

About a year had passed and one day while thinking about these family meetings, the Lord spoke to me and said, *"In having these family meetings, you are painting a picture in Jonathan and Jessica's hearts of humility, accountability, and submission."* It was so exciting to hear this from the Lord, but at the same time sobering. Exciting, because of how powerful these three character traits are when operating in a person's life. Sobering, as I realized the awesome responsibility of being a parent and how our actions and behavior patterns paint pictures, good or bad, in the hearts and minds of our children. There may still be things that Jonathan and/or Jessica may have been hurt by or internalized during their formative years from significant others (i.e., me, their dad, their teachers, or peers) where they may need healing and to forgive. If so, I'm confident that the Lord, through their own relationship with Him, will be faithful to reveal them. I also could see as I continued to exercise humility in my own life, it was dealing with the evil tendency of pride and arrogance on the inside of me. However, I still was not walking in victory, meaning I wasn't producing the fruit that comes from walking in the new man in Christ, the born-again creation (e.g., love, joy, peace, longsuffering, gentleness, goodness, faith, meekness, temperance – Galatians 5:22-24). After going through Christian counseling and *Living Waters*, there were two major areas of concern that I still had:

1. On two separate occasions, I found myself intrigued by an attractive woman who seemed very <u>strong and confident in her personhood</u>, one on

television and the other on the cover of a CD, and I was drawn to them. I was concerned about what I was feeling, so I went before the Lord with it. He spoke to me and said, "It can't come through any other woman but your mother." In other words, my mom was foundational in my own gender security and no other woman could give me what only my mom could have. We can certainly grow in gender wholeness through healthy same-sex friendships as long as we are foundationally secure (see an example on page 47). It confirmed to me that I was drawn to women who seemed confident in their femininity due to the lack of my own. Here is some information about my birth and some history leading up to it that I believe was a factor that contributed to my lack of feminine strength.

When my mom was pregnant with my sister, she was hoping she was pregnant with a boy and was disappointed when she found out she wasn't. As a baby, my sister was very demanding; therefore, Mom decided that she did not want another child. Dad continued to convince her otherwise and finally succeeded. Months after I was conceived, during a routine doctor's visit, the doctor listened to my heartbeat and said that it was so strong that I would probably be a football player. This gave Mom hope that I was going to be the boy she wanted. After I was born, I'm sure she was disappointed that I was not a boy and on top of that she was pretty depleted. We had been home from the hospital for about a week when she began bleeding due to complications from my birth. Dad took my sister and me to stay with my grandmother and took Mom back to the hospital. After examining her, they found that infection had set in from using unsterile instruments during my delivery. There wasn't anything they could do and prepared dad for the worst. She was in the hospital for two weeks and Dad thought he was going to lose her. Her one request to him was, "Take care of my babies." While my sister and I were at my grandmother's house, I was told that I would not stop crying, so much so that the doctor was called. Back then, doctors made house calls, and when he arrived at the house and examined me he said, "She misses her mother." Throughout my formative years, I needed more of her nurturing heart than she had the grace or the ability to give to me (e.g., patient and tender attentiveness, teaching, and instruction through interaction in play and household activites). I believe this also contributed to the deep need that I had for a woman's love and touch at a very young age.

2. One morning in the early part of 2000 as I was before the Lord, I said, "Lord, I don't understand why I am not producing fruit in my life like I should. As much time as I spend with you, and after going through this extensive time of inner healing, I still find myself being controlled by anger and becoming defensive, especially toward my husband. Why don't I see the spiritual fruit in my life?"

   It was then the Lord began to zero in on my behavior patterns, exposing the deep-seated root of rebellion He revealed to me while going through the *Living Waters Program*. I was unaware at the time, but the Lord was about to reveal a protective covering in me that needed to be removed. The Lord's desire was to remove everything in me that was keeping the new creation from operating in my life. His desire is for all of his children to be deeply rooted and grounded in His love and nothing else (Ephesians 3:14-21; Colossians 2:6-7). He began by giving me a dream.

   In the dream, Jesus was walking around in my temple (we are the temple of the Holy Spirit – 1 Corinthians 6:19). As He was walking around, I was seeing what He was seeing. Everything was clean and spotless! There were several oblong tables with white tablecloths reaching to the floor. As He was walking around, He walked over to one of the tables and as He was pulling up the tablecloth, He said, "Everything looks good, but we've got to get rid of this." Underneath the table was an animal about the size of a fox with short brown fur curled up asleep with its back to me. (Nothing is hidden from the Lord!)

I also realized that this is what dropped in me when I was in my early twenties while my dad and I were outside in his backyard (**Part One**). It's important to note, that this animal came from the "deep-seated root of rebellion" operating within me, as I had walked away from the Lord at the age of twenty.

Several weeks went by and the Lord began to bring revelation to me concerning the consequence of this deep-seated root of rebellion. Here is what happened:

During this time, Don was a homebuilder. Around 2001, he was building a house and renovating an older home he had purchased for resale. At the home he was renovating, the backyard had apple trees and peach trees in full bloom. I decided to pick the fruit and make some apple pies and peach pies, and bless people with them.

As I was in the kitchen making the pies, Jonathan and Jessica saw the peach pits on the kitchen counter and asked if we could plant them? Later that week, I got some very small pots at the recycle center and purchased some rich potting soil. The next day the three of us went outside and began planting those peach pits. We put the pots on top of our well so they could get the sun and the rain they needed in order to grow.

Two or three weeks went by and nothing was coming out of the soil, so one day, while Jonathan was at school, I said to Jessica, "Let's get one of those pots and dig around in the soil and find out what's going on in there!" We got one of the small pots and began to dig in the soil until we found the pit and it looked exactly like it did when we planted it. I said to Jessica, "Look, it hasn't done anything! Go get me the nutcracker and let's crack this thing open." When she came back with the nutcracker, I cracked it open and inside was the seed! I said, "Jessica," holding the shell in one hand and the seed in the other, "this isn't the seed, this is the seed!" So, we planted the seed in the pot with the rich potting soil and set it on the well, and one week later a twig popped out of the soil. We were so excited! I then realized that the Lord wanted to show me a spiritual truth in this but I didn't see it right off. A few days later, as I was in prayer, the Lord reminded me of the peach pit and said, "That's its protective covering!"

That was all He had to say! I understood that peach pit was protecting that seed from falling into the ground in order to die to become the tree it was created to become and to produce the fruit it was created to produce. It had all the right ingredients to grow to be the peach tree it was created to be; but it could not as long as that protective covering was surrounding it (John 12:24-25). I could clearly see the parallel of how I had been defending myself in my own strength with my carnal weapon (my tongue) and why I was not bearing fruit. My defense mechanisms (e.g., anger, argumentativeness, protecting my right-to-be-right, defiance), the protective covering—the old man – Colossians 3:8-9, which was protecting my heart from being hurt, was keeping the born-again creation, the new man, from coming forth and producing spiritual fruit (Galatians 5:22-25)!

I wanted to be like Christ, but until that protective covering was removed, it was not going to happen! In the same way that peach pit had to be removed from that seed, the Lord was showing me that the deep-seated root of rebellion and all that was associated with it, including the animal He had revealed to me in the dream, had to be removed from me. I didn't know how that was going to happen; but I knew if He revealed it to me, He would be faithful to remove it from me. The Lord also used two incidents to show me this deep-seated root of rebellion.

1. One afternoon Don was downstairs in his office working on tax returns. He called out to me and asked me to come and help him with our taxes. As I was sitting across the desk from him, I was thinking to myself, "He better not try to tell me how to do this!" At that moment, the Lord spoke to me and said, "<u>You're argumentative</u>!" I was taken aback a little bit, and I immediately shared with Don what the Lord said. Don said, "It's that rebellion working in you." I didn't comment on that statement, but when I got before the Lord the next morning, I began to do a word study on "argumentative" so I could fully own the behavior before I took it to the Lord in repentance.

2. A few days later, I was on the phone with my dad, and he said something that I didn't agree with. I said something back to him, and then said, "Bye!" and hung up the phone. Immediately the Lord spoke to me and said, "<u>You're defiant</u>!" I quickly called my dad back and apologized to him. As I was before the Lord, I spent time looking up the word "defiance" and the synonyms associated with it, writing all of them down so that I could fully own that behavior before I took it to Him in repentance. One definition for defiance is "a daring or bold resistance to authority or to any opposing force."[2]

I want to remind the reader again of the definition of deep-seated. The word "deep-seated" is defined as "existing for a long time and very difficult to change: firmly established."[3]

Several months later, the Lord gave me a directive, and my obedience to that directive would forever change my life: In October 2002, He spoke to me and said, "I want four mornings a week for six months." Again, because of my reverence for Him, I complied with His request. Each morning after returning home from taking Jonathan and Jessica to school, I would go downstairs into my prayer area. I would begin by giving thanks to the Lord and worshipping Him. I would then journal to Him any cares, fears, concerns, anger, etc., I may have been struggling with (1 Peter 5:6-9). After a week of reading His Word, giving thanks to Him, and prayer, the Lord began to direct me to personalize certain portions of Scripture concerning who He is in relationship to me, and portions of Scripture concerning putting off the old man and putting on the new man in Christ. Thank God that He is the same yesterday, today, and forever; His will for us never changes (Hebrews 13:8; Malachi 3:6)! During my prayer time, after a couple of weeks of confessing aloud these personalized Scriptures and continuing to journal my concerns, worries, anger, and frustrations (i.e., the old man) to Him, it literally began to change my life; as I was putting off the old man and putting on the new man in Christ (Galatians 3:27). The Lord began using my tongue to "skillfully" write on my heart a picture of the "new man" by using specific portions of Scripture. Please see Scripture references below:

- Psalm 45:1 – *...my tongue is the pen of a ready writer.* The word "ready" in Hebrew is *mahiyr* meaning "quick; hence, skillful: diligent, hasty, ready."
- Proverbs 7:1-3 (NKJV) – *My son, keep my words, and treasure my commands within you. Keep my commands and live, and my law as the apple of your eye. Bind them on your fingers; write them on the tablet of your heart.*
- 2 Corinthians 3:2-3 (NKJV) – *...clearly you are an epistle of Christ, ministered by us, written not with ink but by the Spirit of the living God, not on tablets of stone but on tablets of flesh, that is, of the heart.*

Through this process, I began to find it easier to trust the Lord during challenging times, and I also found a renewed strength to perform my responsibilities as a stay-at-home mom and housewife with joy instead of duty. Don had no idea that I had been spending four mornings a week with the Lord. One afternoon, about six weeks into this spiritual exercise, he and I were sitting in the living room waiting on Jonathan and Jessica to come home from school. He said to me, "I just want you to know that all the resentment and bitterness that I have had toward you is washing away." This was the beginning of seeing the fruit of my time downstairs, changing my spiritual clothing, putting off the old man and putting on the new man in Christ. I said to myself, "Lord, You are amazing! Only You know how to make marriages work!" The Lord then began to reveal to me truths in His Word that I share throughout the ***Scripture Guide Study Notes - Volume 2***.

One afternoon in February 2003, four months into the Lord's directive, I was home alone in my kitchen and all of a sudden, the best way that I can describe it is, I felt an opening up within me and a true connection with the Lord, a wellspring of life (John 7:38). When this happened, I gasped and said, "This is it! This is what everybody is looking for! How can I help others get here?" ***Character Development in Christ*** is the answer to that prayer. I could see how the Lord used the power, purity, and life of His Word, to dismantle the ingrained carnal core beliefs and mindsets that had become strongholds in my life (Psalm 12:6, 119:9; Ecclesiastes 8:4; Ephesians 5:25-27). He also used His Word and the power of His Spirit to remove the deep-seated root of rebellion and all that was associated with it (i.e., the animal He had shown me the year prior in the dream where He said, "We need to get rid of this!"). When it was removed, I gasped because of the change I literally felt on the inside. The Lord showed me that when I walked away from Him at the age of twenty, it opened the door to the enemy of my soul, Satan, and because of this deep-seated root of rebellion, my heart was hardened with this animal which kept the Lord's living water and the fruit of His Spirit from becoming a reality in my life. I haven't been the same since! This caused such a transformation within me that it was like a caterpillar who instinctively wraps itself in its cocoon and through a secret process called metamorphosis, comes out as a butterfly! Only the born-again creation can overcome the carnal nature within us and its behavior patterns, *"Can the Ethiopian change his skin, or the leopard his spots? Then may ye also do good, that are accustomed to do evil"* (Jeremiah 13:23). What I could not do within my own self to change my behavior patterns, the Lord did—by His Word and through the power of His Spirit! The born-again creation has become a reality in my life!

As I shared in Chapter 1 about the correlation between the kidney and the *inmost mind*, I could clearly see what happened to me. As the Lord directed me to personalize certain Scriptures, speaking them aloud "and receiving them as my own," the power, purity, and life of His Word began to enter into my *inmost mind*. As the kidneys remove toxic waste from the blood to keep the body healthy; in the same way the *inmost mind*, as the life of His Word became a consistent flow, began to filter and flush out ingrained carnal core beliefs and mindsets or toxic waste (e.g., rebellion, pride, insecurities, rejection), the primary source of the old man (Leviticus 17:11; John 6:63; Ephesians 5:25-27; 1 Peter 1:22-23, 3:1-4). Hallelujah! These Scriptures are now compiled in the **Personalized Scripture Guide**, Chapter 4.

About a week after this protective covering was removed, the Lord helped me to see just how powerful this defining moment was for me. Here is what happened:

> Don and I had committed to take care of a couple of teenagers for the weekend while their grandparents were out of town. The four of us sat down for supper. Jonathan and Jessica were not with us that evening. Don made a derogatory comment about the meal I had prepared and it made me very angry. I slammed my hand down on the kitchen table and got everybody's attention and to my surprise and amazement,

nothing came out! There wasn't anything on the inside of me to beat him up with! So, I just shrugged my shoulders and we all went back to eating and talking about other things.

The next day we were talking to the two teenagers and sharing about Christ and I shared with them what took place at the supper table. One of the teenagers responded with, "How did you keep from saying anything?" I said, "It was God! He cleaned my house (Titus 3:4-7)! Hallelujah!"

A few days later, I felt led to go on a 40-day fast much like I imagined Adam and Eve ate while in the garden (e.g., fruits, vegetables, nuts, grains). During that fast, the Lord gave me the name, ***Character Development in Christ***, and at the end of the fast He spoke to me and asked me to fast a tenth of each year. I have been doing that ever since. During the next four years (2004-2007) at the end of each fast, the Lord gave me more insight as to the formation of the ***Personalized Scripture Guide***. After that, He became silent concerning this work. Eight years later in 2015, one spring day while I was in my kitchen, the Lord spoke to me and said, "It's time." For the next five years He helped me to complete it, and I give Him much thanks! In 2016, while working on the book, the Lord spoke to me one morning and said, "I want to speak" (1 Corinthians 12:1-11). He then began to give me "words of wisdom" for each portion of Scripture contained in the ***Personalized Scripture Guide***. These "words of wisdom" are now included with the guide, entitled *Heart-to-heart*.

Since February 2003, the wellspring of His living water has produced much fruit in my life. I'm not talking about having a large ministry; I'm referring to my relationships at home, with others, and myself. Here are some examples:

My husband: It was no longer a drudgery to serve and honor Don as I began to serve him and my family as unto the Lord. To this day, the energy level, peace, and joy that I have to perform my tasks, at times, amazes me (Ephesians 5:22; Nehemiah 8:10; Romans 14:17). I released Don from my control and expectations and surrendered those to the Lord, and I now operate out of a place of faith, hope, and love (1 Corinthians 13:13). Although Don and I still have moments of frustration with each other, I began to appreciate my husband and his desire for excellence. I appreciate the fact that he was and is present to me and to our children. He is always available to us when we need to talk and to run things by him, and he always counsels us with wisdom from God's Word. My respect and love for him increases as we walk together in God's grace. I respect the fact that he is a man of prayer and one who stands in the truth of God's Word.

<u>My children</u>: The Lord could trust me even more with our children, as children are very precious to Him (Mark 10:14). Before He removed the protective covering from me, Jonathan and Jessica were better off being taught in public school than being taught by me, because of the narcissistic stronghold of pride and my lack of patience. Because of the work Christ accomplished within me, He moved in both Don and me to homeschool Jonathan and Jessica, and for four years I did. I found myself enjoying spending time with them during the day and I saw the fruit of gentleness and patience operating within me. I was also able to teach them more about Christ throughout the day.

<u>Others</u>: Soon after this defining moment took place in my life, my mother-in-law moved into our basement apartment. On one occasion when I was dealing with some anger toward her, I decided to journal those feelings of anger to the Lord and He immediately instructed me to go clean her apartment. I thought to myself, "Really?!," as that certainly was not what I felt like doing! As I began cleaning her apartment, the love of God washed away the anger that I had felt and replaced it with His love for her. The love and respect that I have for others is very real to me.

<u>Myself</u>: Since February 2003, after the protective covering which kept His living water from flowing within me was removed, the completion, security, and wholeness that I had been lacking and searching for most of my adult life through His creation—woman, was fulfilled by His living water. The born-again creation became a reality within me and I became totally free from same-sex attraction! Because of the healing and transformation that has taken place within me, when I talk about my past it's like I'm talking about somebody else. Hallelujah! I now have a deeper understanding as to what the Lord said to the Samaritan woman at the well in John 4:6-18. She had a deep need in her that she tried to satisfy through men. She had been married five times and the man that she was presently living with was not her husband. Jesus was

offering her something that no one and nothing could satisfy, His living water that would fill the deep longings of her heart. Also, as I mentioned earlier that we can certainly grow in gender wholeness through healthy same-sex friendships, I would like to give an example. In the latter part of 2007, after enrolling Jonathan and Jessica in a Christian school, the Lord prompted me to start a house cleaning business. This would allow me to be able to take Jonathan and Jessica to school in the morning, go to work, and finish in time to pick them up after school in the afternoon. Since I began my business in 2008, a strong bond has formed between me and several of my female clients while working closely together on home projects. Through these relationships, I continued to grow in gender strength and security as I beheld their own. However, the strength, security, and confidence of living out of the new man in Christ—my true self, far surpasses any strength, security, and confidence found in gender, race, ethnicity, heritage... *"For as many of you as have been baptized into Christ have put on Christ. There is neither Jew nor Greek, there is neither bond nor free, there is neither male nor female: for ye are all one in Christ Jesus"* (Galatians 3:27-28).

I have also found that as my carnal core beliefs and mindsets have changed through renewing the *spirit of my mind* or my *inmost mind* to the truth of God's Word, the feelings and emotions associated with those carnal beliefs (i.e., low self-esteem, lack of self-worth or value) have diminished. Instead of a narcissistic stronghold of pride and deep feelings of insecurity and self-rejection, the Lord and His truth have become my stronghold and strength (Psalm 18:2; Proverbs 10:29; Nahum 1:7)! When I do find myself feeling hurt, angry, or fearful, it only takes a few minutes for the Lord's peace to override those feelings. Therefore, the need to journal feelings of anger to Him has become less and less.

Because of the deep work Christ has done within me, by removing the protective covering and the mental strongholds concerning myself and others that caused so much pain in my life, anger no longer has control over me. What is now operating within me, empowered by the *spirit of my mind* or my *inmost mind*, are godly beliefs concerning righteousness and true holiness, the new man (Ephesians 4:22-23) or as 1 Peter 3:4 describes, *"The hidden man of the heart!"* Hallelujah! I am now living out of a place of peace, quietness, and assurance and the joy of the Lord is truly my strength (Isaiah 32:17; Nehemiah 8:10)!

My trust is in Jesus Christ, not in myself, my husband, others, or things. By His Word and the power of His Spirit, He continues His work within me, teaching me how to function and operate out of my true self—who I am in Christ. I found that by speaking aloud the portions of Scriptures contained in the ***Personalized Scripture Guide***, "<u>and receiving them as my own</u>," His Words painted a picture on the inside of me, a new image of myself, how present the Father is to me, and how I am to treat others. By the Word of His grace, I am able to see clearly how to walk in this new image as His Spirit enlightens my soul (2 Corinthians 3:3, 17-18). I am walking in a new sense of being; for it is truly in Him that we live and move and have our being (Acts 17:28)!

As I continue to speak aloud these Scriptures on a regular basis, it keeps the born-again creation fresh in my conscious thinking and continues to provide spiritual strength and nourishment to my inner man (Ephesians 4:22-24; 1 Peter 1:22-2:3; 1 Corinthians 3:1-3; John 6:35, 7:37-39). Let me be clear, this does not mean that I am perfect in all that I do or say as this is certainly not the case. What it does mean is that I am very conscious of my vulnerabilities and when I do fall short I am quick to repent as the strength of the new man within me has now become stronger than my flesh or carnal nature (see ***Scripture Guide Study Notes - Volume 2***, Note 27b, for a revelation of this from the Old Testament). Since February 2003, the Lord has also revealed other things within me such as judgments toward others and other carnal thought patterns that I needed to repent of and release to Him (see ***Scripture Guide Study Notes - Volume 2***, Note 27a, for an example; this example is also included in the ***Personal Prayer Journal – Details and Instructions***, Chapter 5). The reality of the Lord's presence has become a reality in my heart. I understand my role as His daughter and I am able to take on that responsibility because it is Christ in me. I understand now, that He truly is my Covering and my Strength, He truly is my Rock and my Salvation, and He truly is my Shield and my Fortress. He truly is my Counselor. He truly is my Father, and He truly cares for me! Amen!

Chapter 3

DON'S TESTIMONY

"I will sing of the mercy and loving-kindness of the Lord forever; with my mouth will I make known Your faithfulness from generation to generation" (Psalm 89:1, AMPCE).

It is with the greatest of joy and pleasure, my privilege and honor to declare to all, the works of Christ Jesus of which He accomplished on Calvary's Cross for my life. In my spirit, even now, I can hear Him crying, "IT IS FINISHED." I can almost see clearly Him looking down at me as I kneel before Him at the cross. With confidence in His eyes, He assures me that life is glorious, that His ways will be revealed to me. His tears, His agony, and anguish and pain, which were mine to bear, He willfully bore, my sin and it's reproach He bore. My grief and sorrow He himself also bore. The wrath, judgment, and punishment for my sin was poured out upon Him.

Do I love Him? I tell you I would be frightened without end without Him. He is my salvation; He has become my comfort and source of strength. Every breath I draw earnestly seems to bring greater hope and peace as I look to Him.

I write freely to you that Christ Jesus be lifted up. And without shame or fear of rejection, I can honestly reveal to you my testimony. The works of God as revealed in the creation of the heavens, the earth, and man are incredibly great. I feel that even greater is the work of God revealed in the redemption of man through Christ:

As a child, there was much unrest in my little soul. My father, an alcoholic and a very broken man, was unfaithful to my mother, my sister, and me. He drank without concern whether we had food to eat. He chased women. Needless to say, he abandoned us at a very early age. The only memories of my father are flashes involving physical abuse. At age two, Mother informed my father at the only place she could find him (a bar) that she could take no more. I screamed and cried as we left the bar and walked the sidewalk. I wanted my broken daddy to hold me in his arms. Fifteen years later, I saw him again in a casket, which the state of Michigan provided.

At age five, my mother remarried a man she was confident would remain faithful to her, my sister, and me. He did not drink or smoke nor go to church. My mother worked weekends to help support us. Soon after their marriage, mother had a third child (a girl). My adopted father grew very partial to her, and soon when Mother was away working, I again began to experience the verbal and physical abuse. There were many threats made on my life, as well as my sister's life. He, at times, threatened to kill us if we ever opened our mouths. As we grew enough to know that the iron skillet on his head might save our soul, we began to open our mouths. At age seventeen, my mother divorced him and within six months remarried the third time.

Needless to say, deep within I began to deal with a genuine emptiness within my soul. I sought comfort in many forms to satisfy the gnawing, aching pain, and confusion. The need for affirmation was overwhelming. I quickly began seeking what I assumed to be liberty or freedom, possibly even joy. My search began in a girlfriend of three years. She could not offer me what I desperately needed and what was never imparted through relationship with my father or stepfathers. I soon found myself seeking to satisfy my need and identity in men. For eight years I lived in my own hell because no man was able to fulfill my hunger. They too all failed me. They did not, nor could not, fill my depravation. I bought many cars – often annually – clothing, jewelry, homes, etc. With each new relationship, or object, I would find temporary relief from the pain, the rejection, the shame, and last but not least, the fear.

At age 25, I was diagnosed with high blood pressure. The alcohol and anger combined were like a bottle pressurized, ready to blow. The anger and wrath that I was subjected to as a child caused me to defensively detach. I made many inner vows as I did not know how to deal rationally with my anger. I did not want to be angry like my fathers. I became a victim of my own judgments, and I became a slave, seeking laboriously to earn any and every man's love and approval.

BUT God, in his infinite wisdom and mercy came to me one evening late as I left a gay bar. I repented and acknowledged my need and brokenness to Him. He manifested His presence, His love, and will for me in an audible voice; I was struck with awe that He knew me and so gently loved me. I opened my mouth and verbally declared, "Of a truth, thou art the Living God." Two weeks later He again spoke to me audibly in a swimming pool as I, for the first time apart from the corporate anointing, offered the sacrifice of thanksgiving. He said He loved me and He would give me a baby boy with beautiful blue eyes. Wow, that warm summer evening late in the starlight and moonlight, our love affair began. His perfect love so quickly began to dispel the fear, which tormented me day and night. He led me, as I prayed, to a small church where I again was amazed. People praised God freely. There was a sense of victory, which filled the sanctuary. I abandoned my hopelessness and dove into the river of God – headfirst. He blessed me within two years with my precious wife, Christy. My promised first-born son, Jonathan, and my precious little Jessica. My lover and Savior continues to give me the desires of my heart. I love Him always and make my boast in Him.

Nearly thirty-five years have passed since that moonlit night, and in His love and mercy, He has walked me through many fires and deep waters. I love His discipline. I know it is born out of pure love. I cry out to Him often to free me to live, to love, and to serve. He has faithfully revealed my deep wounds and healed them. It's not magic, it's His pure love. I have found the freedom which comes with confession and repentance (James 5:16). I found it was not necessarily my abuser's fault that my heart had become so hard and defiled. My sinful reaction defiled my soul as well.

I realize God has given validity to my pain through Christ. I know now He was with me all along in the Garden of Gethsemane, as well as the cross, where he beforehand identified with my suffering. And yes, I am satisfied with the vengeance He exacted or executed upon my enemies. He poured it out upon my Savior, Jesus, at Calvary. Now I am free to love you and my broken daddies.

Some of you, whether broken sexually through homosexuality or heterosexually, might ask, "Is it really all so easy, Don?" I would respond honestly by saying, "No, not necessarily; not in your own strength." I would guess it would be near to impossible. There are many who never act out sexually their fantasies or act out their brokenness. Yet the roots still exist or remain. It is by God's grace, I believe, I have been able honestly to resist temptations, until God revealed my gender insecurities, at their root. I have learned that I cannot trust my feelings. I can trust God with His Word and love. My focus is on Him, not my false identity. He alone has given me new form and definition. No longer does shame, rejection and fear name me. God has removed the reproach of my sin (guilt and shame). I know nearly as well as my Father in heaven now who I am. I am free. I am His own. Sin has lost its power and victory over me. Death no longer reigns in me. But Christ liveth in me. Can I sin sexually again? Yes, if I choose. But I have already a man and God in Christ. Also, my friend and godly wife, Christy. In Christ's strength, I continue to stand and honor them.

Cry out to Him, He will answer you and deliver you. "As for God, His way is perfect! The word of the Lord is tested and tried; He is a shield to all those who take refuge and put their trust in Him" (Psalm 18:30, AMPCE).

God Bless you,

Don Morgan

Chapter 4

PERSONALIZED SCRIPTURE GUIDE
Details and Directives

Details:
I would like to begin by sharing what I believe to be a parallel from something that took place in the Old Testament with what took place within me when the born-again creation became a reality in my life. First, here is some background information:

In Genesis 29-31, Jacob had served Laban twenty years, fourteen years for his two daughters, Leah and Rachel, and six years for his cattle (Genesis 31:41). However, Laban was not upright in his dealings with Jacob as described below:

1. Jacob served Laban the first seven years for his daughter, Rachel. Afterwards, when the seven years of service was accomplished, instead of giving Rachel to Jacob, Laban gave him his eldest daughter, Leah (Genesis 29:16-27). In Genesis 29:26-28, after Jacob confronted Laban about it, Laban said, *"It must not be done so in our country, to give the younger before the firstborn. Fulfill her week, and we will give thee this also for the service which thou shalt serve with me yet seven other years."* And, so, Jacob did.

2. Labon changed Jacob's wages ten times (Genesis 31:41).

3. After twenty years of service, in Genesis 30:25-26, Jacob went to Laban and said, *"Send me away, that I may go unto my own place, and to my country. Give me my wives and my children, for whom I have served thee, and let me go..."* Laban said, *"Name me your wages, and I will give it"* (Genesis 30:28-NKJV). In Genesis 30:32, Jacob said that he wanted all the speckled and spotted sheep, and all the brown ones among the sheep, and the spotted and speckled among the goats: and of such shall be my hire. Laban agreed, but, on that same day, Laban removed the male goats that were speckled and spotted, and all the female goats that were speckled and

spotted, and every one that had some white in it, and all the brown ones among the sheep, and gave them to his sons (Genesis 30:34-35). In Genesis 30:37-39, God gave Jacob wisdom to do the following:

And Jacob took him rods of green poplar, and of the hazel and chesnut (chestnut) tree; and pilled (peeled) white strakes in them, and made the white appear which was in the rods. And he set the rods which he had pilled (peeled) before the flocks in the gutters in the watering troughs when the flocks came to drink, that they should conceive when they came to drink. And the flocks conceived before the rods, and brought forth cattle ringstraked (streaked), speckled, and spotted.

As I shared in **My Story – Part Two**, after twenty years of seeking the Lord but still stuck in my old carnal behavior patterns and mindsets, the Lord, too, gave me wisdom to cause the born-again creation within me to become a reality in my life. He separated me for a season (four mornings a week for six months) to commune with Him, the fountain of living waters (Psalm 36:9; Jeremiah 2:13, 17:13; Revelation 21:6). During this time, He led me to personalize portions of Scripture from God's trees of righteousness (holy men of God who penned the holy Scriptures) relating to the born-again creation (Isaiah 61:3; 2 Peter 1:20-21). I continued to gaze and drink in these truths, as I spoke them forth four times a week, and in four months something amazing took place within me as the born-again creation in Christ became a reality in my life! Hallelujah! These portions of Scripture are now compiled in this guide for your benefit, as it is our heavenly Father's desire for all of His children to live out of this new creation, the new man in Christ.

This Scripture guide is the heart of **Character Development in Christ**. It is divided into three sections described below. Each portion of Scripture is numbered [i.e., 1(a), (b), (c), (d), (e); 2(a), (b)...] to coincide with the **Scripture Guide Study Notes - Volume 2**, expounding these Scriptures with personal notes, teachings, insights, and over 6,000 Scripture quotations, many repetitive. Also included in the Scripture guide are "words of wisdom" from the Lord entitled *Heart-to-heart*. Why *Heart-to-heart*? In 2016, while working on the book, the Lord spoke to me one morning and said, "I want to speak" (1 Corinthians 12:1-11). He then began giving me "words of wisdom" for one or two portions of Scripture each week.

Part One – Putting off the old man contains twelve portions of Scripture including "words of wisdom" from the Lord entitled *Heart-to-heart*. It is designed to help renew the *spirit of your mind* or your *inmost mind* (1) to your heavenly Father's eternal love, care, and faithfulness toward you, and (2) to the importance of casting your cares, anxieties, and distractions upon Him because He cares for you (1 Peter 5:6-9). The AMPCE Version calls these thorn plants that choke the Word of God, making it unfruitful (Mark 4:7, 14, 18-19). As long as we are in these earthen vessels, we must surrender these to the Lord, as a gardener removes weeds from his garden.

Part Two – Putting off the old man contains six portions of Scripture including "words of wisdom" from the Lord entitled *Heart-to-heart*. It is designed to help renew the *spirit of your mind* or your *inmost mind* (1) to your heavenly Father's eternal love, care, and faithfulness toward you, and (2) to the importance of keeping your mind stayed on Him and refraining from behavior originating from the old man. The AMPCE Version also calls these thorn plants that choke the Word of God making it unfruitful (Mark 4:7, 14, 18-19). Jesus said in Luke 9:23 (NKJV), *"If anyone desires to come after Me, let him deny himself, and take up his cross daily, and follow Me."*

Part Three – Putting off the old man and putting on the new man in Christ contains thirty-two portions of Scripture including "words of wisdom" from the Lord entitled *Heart-to-heart*. It is designed to help renew the *spirit of your mind* or your *inmost mind* (1) to your heavenly Father's eternal love, care, and faithfulness toward you, and (2) to the new man in Christ. It also reveals the carnal behavior patterns and mindsets of the old man. Victory in Christ is obtained as we choose to put off the old man, be renewed in the *spirit of our minds*, and put on the new man which after God is created in righteousness and true holiness (Ephesians 4:17-24; James 1:22-25).

Renewing the *spirit of your mind* or your *inmost mind* to the new man, the born-again creation within, has no definitive time frame. It takes as long as it takes for the repetitive process to begin to change the patterns of carnal thinking. As you do this, I believe you will begin to see real change take place in your life. God told Joshua,

> *"This Book of the Law shall not depart from your mouth, but you shall meditate in it day and night, that you may observe to do according to all that is written in it. For then you will make your way prosperous, and then you will have good success."*
> (Joshua 1:8, NKJV)

As your heart and tongue are connected, this process of repetitively speaking aloud the faith-filled words contained in this Scripture guide, allows the Word of God to change your internal belief system, which is holding you captive to the old man or carnal nature. During this spiritual exercise, you are using your tongue as a pen and taking the Word of God, as it relates to your heavenly Father's eternal love, care, and faithfulness toward you and to the new man in Christ, and literally writing that image upon the table of your heart by the Spirit of the living God (Luke 6:45; Psalm 15:1-5, 45:1; Proverbs 3:1-3, 7:2-3; 2 Corinthians 3:3; Hebrews 4:12-14).

Through this renewal process, a picture of the new man whose trust and confidence is in God's eternal love and care, is painted upon your heart, and you will then begin to clearly see how to walk in it as the Holy Spirit enlightens your soul. Also, as the Word of God is living and powerful and sharper than any two-edged sword, the Lord uses His Word, by the power of His Spirit, to circumcise the foreskin of your heart, removing the carnality (e.g., worldliness and carnal mindsets, judgments, strongholds, protective coverings), which is keeping the new man from coming forth (Hebrews 4:12-13; Romans 2:28-29; Colossians 2:6-15). Please refer to the ***Scripture Guide Study Notes - Volume 2***, Note 33b, for more information and Scripture references concerning the heart and the tongue. To better understand the importance of this, below are four analogies:

1. The Word of God is compared to seed and to water (Mark 4:14; Ephesians 5:26; Titus 3:5). When you plant the Word of God in your heart, it is like planting seed into the ground. If your heart ground is polluted/defiled through sin, it can only be cleansed through repentance (acknowledging the behavior as sin, asking the Lord for forgiveness, and then turning from that particular behavior of the old man to the new man in Christ – Matthew 15:10-20; 1 John 1:7-9; Ephesians 5:26; Titus 3:5). You are responsible for dealing with your old man through prayer, repentance, and planting His Words of truth in your heart by renewing the *spirit of your mind* or your *inmost mind* (Ephesians 4:20-24). As you do this, the seed of His Word begins to grow, changing you from the inside out. As you do your part, the Lord, through His Word and by His Spirit, is faithful to bring you victory over the old man and freedom in Christ (Hebrew 4:12-14; John 8:31-36). As you speak aloud these personalized Scriptures, as outlined below in the first directive, it is like watering and nurturing the born-again incorruptible seed that is within you and God is faithful to give the increase (1 Peter 1:22-2:3; 1 Corinthians 3:5-7). This process takes time, as Jesus said,

> *"...So is the kingdom of God, as if a man should cast seed into the ground; and should sleep, and rise night and day, and the seed should spring and grow up, he knoweth not how. For the earth bringeth forth fruit of herself; first the blade, then the ear, after that the full corn in the ear. But when the fruit is brought forth, immediately he putteth in the sickle, because the harvest is come."* And he said, *"Whereunto shall we liken the kingdom of God? Or with what comparison shall we compare it? It is like a grain of mustard seed, which, when it is sown in the earth; is less than all the seeds that be in the earth; but when it is sown, it groweth up, and becometh greater than all herbs, and shooteth out great branches; so that the fowls of the air may lodge under the shadow of it."*
>
> (Mark 4:1-32)

Based on this passage of Scripture it is important to remember two facts: (1) It takes time for spiritual growth to occur, just as it takes time for a seed planted in the ground to grow into a mature plant. (2) As you are speaking aloud these faith-filled words, it's going deeper than your conscious thinking. Therefore, your part is to plant and water God's Word and to continue to go about your day-to-day life with an expectation of spiritual growth. The Lord's part is to cause His Word to grow and bring forth fruit in your life (1 Corinthians 3:1-6; Galatians 5:22-23). Through this process, I am confident that He will reveal any strongholds, judgments, or hardness of heart within you that needs to be removed through repentance in order for your heart ground to be able to produce fruit from His good seed (Mark 4:1-32; 1 Corinthians 3:5-7). But know this, tribulation (i.e., pressure, affliction, anguish, trouble) and persecution comes because of the Word and we enter into the kingdom through much tribulation; so do not be discouraged and give up when you encounter hardships (Matthew 13:20-21; John 16:33; Acts 14:22; Romans 8:35-39; 2 Thessalonians 1:4-10). Continue to allow the Word of God to take root within your heart and mind through spiritual strength training by being a doer of the Word (Ephesians 3:17-21; Colossians 2:7; 1 Timothy 4:7-8; James 1:22-25). See **Scripture Guide Study Notes - Volume 2**, Note 4a, for details.

2. Paul said,

> *"I beseech you therefore, brethren, by the mercies of God, that you present your bodies a living sacrifice, holy, acceptable to God, which*

is your reasonable service. And do not be conformed to this world, but be <u>transformed</u> by the renewing of your mind, that you may prove what is that good and acceptable and perfect will of God."
(Romans 12:1-2, NKJV)

The word "transformed" in the Greek is *metamorphoo*. Its meaning in the Thayer's Greek Lexicon is "to change into another form, to transfigure, transform: of Christians: we are transformed into the same image (of consummate excellence that shines in Christ), reproduce the same image, 2 Corinthians 3:18; used of the change of moral character for the better." Does this Greek word sound familiar? The word metamorphosis is a process, for example, that takes place when a caterpillar's form changes into a butterfly. As you choose to renew your mind to the truth of God's Word, true transformation begins to take place within you. The end result is that you will no longer think the same; therefore, you will no longer act the same. God's will for every born-again believer is to be changed into the image of His Son (2 Corinthians 3:17-18). Therefore, this **Personalized Scripture Guide** can be compared to a mirror. As you <u>continue</u>, on a regular basis, speaking aloud these Scriptures along with the "words of wisdom" from the Lord (*Heart-to-heart*), by the Spirit of the living God, you will begin to see clearly how to put off the old man and put on the new man; walking in the perfect law of liberty. What an amazing thing Christ has done for us! Please see the two Scripture references below:

- 2 Corinthians 3:17-18 – *Now the Lord is that Spirit; and where the Spirit of the Lord is, there is liberty. But we all, with open face, beholding as in a glass the glory of the Lord, are changed into the same image from glory to glory, even as by the Spirit of the Lord.*
- James 1:22-25 (NKJV) – *But be doers of the word, and not hearers only, deceiving yourselves. For if anyone is a hearer of the word and not a doer, he is like a man observing his natural face in a mirror; for he observes himself, goes away, and immediately forgets what kind of man he was. But he who looks into the perfect law of liberty and continues in it, and is not a forgetful hearer but a doer of the work, this one will be blessed in what he does.*

3. The Word of God is compared to milk, meat, and the bread of life:

- 1 Peter 2:2-3 – *As newborn babes, desire the sincere milk of the word, that ye may grow thereby: if so be ye have tasted that the Lord is gracious.*

- 1 Corinthians 3:1-3 – *And I, brethren, could not speak unto you as unto spiritual, but as unto carnal, even as unto babes in Christ. I have fed you with milk, and not meat: for hitherto ye were not able to bear it, neither yet now are ye able. For ye are yet carnal: for whereas there is among you envying, and strife, and divisions, are ye not carnal, and walk as men?*
- John 6:35, 51 – *And Jesus said unto them, "I am the bread of life: he that cometh to me shall never hunger; and he that believeth on me shall never thirst. I am the living bread which came down from heaven: if any man eat of this bread, he shall live for ever: and the bread that I will give is my flesh, which I will give for the life of the world."* [John 1:1-3, 14 – *In the beginning was the Word, and the Word was with God, and the Word was God. The same was in the beginning with God. All things were made by him; and without him was not any thing made that was made. <u>And the Word was made flesh, and dwelt among us, (and we beheld his glory, the glory as of the only begotten of the Father,) full of grace and truth</u>*].

Based on these three passages of Scripture, God's Word is spiritual sustenance. Just as God created our bodies to absorb and assimilate the food we ingest. So too as we ingest the Word of God, it provides strength and growth to our inner man, becoming a part of who we are, and enlightens our soul with grace and truth.

4. It is important to remember what I shared about the correlation between the kidneys and the *inmost mind* in Chapter 1 and in ***My Story – Part Two***. Renewing the *spirit of your mind* or your *inmost mind* to the new man, the born-again creation within, has no definitive time frame. It takes as long as it takes for the repetitive process of speaking aloud personalized Scriptures <u>"and receiving them as your own,"</u> for the power, purity, and life of His Word to become a consistent flow into your *inmost mind*. As a reminder, as I shared in Chapter 1, the word "reins" in both the Hebrew and Greek means, "kidney, (figuratively) mind or inmost mind." As the kidneys remove toxic waste from the blood to keep the body healthy; in the same way, the *inmost mind*, as the life of His Word becomes a consistent flow, filters and flushes out ingrained carnal core beliefs and mindsets or toxic waste (e.g., rebellion, pride, insecurities, rejection), the primary source of the old man (Leviticus 17:11; John 6:63; Ephesians 5:25-27; 1 Peter 1:22-23, 3:1-4). As you do this, I believe you will begin to see real change take place in your life (Joshua 1:8).

Directives:

It is important to follow the Lord's leading. As you prayerfully consider the following three directives, I am confident the Lord will reveal to you what He would have you to do:

Directive One

In order to paint a picture of the new man, use this ***Personalized Scripture Guide*** as a mirror to reflect who you truly are in Christ. To provide a consistent flow of the power, purity, and life of God's Word into your *inmost mind*, speak aloud these personalized Scriptures for a season (e.g., three months, six months, nine months):

Day One: Speak aloud the personalized Scriptures along with the corresponding "words of wisdom" from the Lord (*Heart-to-heart*) contained in Part One. Excluding journaling and being quiet before Him, this spiritual exercise takes approximately 15 minutes.

Day Two: Speak aloud the personalized Scriptures along with the corresponding "words of wisdom" from the Lord (*Heart-to-heart*) contained in Part Two. Excluding journaling and being quiet before Him, this spiritual exercise takes approximately 10 minutes.

Day Three: Speak aloud the personalized Scriptures along with the corresponding "words of wisdom" from the Lord (*Heart-to-heart*) contained in Part Three–A, 19-28. Excluding journaling and being quiet before Him, this spiritual exercise takes approximately 10 minutes.

Day Four: Speak aloud the personalized Scriptures along with the corresponding "words of wisdom" from the Lord (*Heart-to-heart*) contained in Part Three–A, 29-37. Excluding journaling and being quiet before Him, this spiritual exercise takes approximately 12 minutes.

Day Five: Speak aloud the personalized Scriptures along with the corresponding "words of wisdom" from the Lord (*Heart-to-heart*) contained in Part Three–B and where applicable, C and D. Excluding journaling and being quiet before Him, this spiritual exercise takes approximately 10-15 minutes.

Repeat this process each week throughout the season the Lord has put upon your heart (e.g., three months, six months, nine months). If you happen to miss a day or a week, don't get upset with yourself, just pick up where you left off. It is also important to keep in mind that this Scripture guide is not intended to be used as a legalistic religious activity, but a vehicle to renew the *spirit of your mind* or your *inmost mind,* and to nourish and strengthen your inner man. I want to encourage you not to be overwhelmed or pressured into thinking you have to complete each day as this guide suggests. As you begin speaking aloud the personalized Scriptures along with the *Heart-to-heart*, allow the Lord to direct you. For example, during Day One, you may be touched by a portion of Scripture or a "word of wisdom" from the Lord (*Heart-to-heart*). You may feel you want to pray or meditate further into this area during the remainder of your time with Him. If this occurs, please do so. The next day, pick up where you left off.

On the other hand, as you spend time familiarizing yourself with the guide and using it for a few weeks, you may find, for example: (1) you would like to speak aloud Day One and Day Two in one sitting, or (2) as in Lisa's case, where she so graciously shared in the last paragraph of her testimony (Exhibit D), the Lord may show you that you need to concentrate on certain portions of Scripture throughout the week where your inner man needs more reinforcement or strength (e.g., Part Three – A. Behavior patterns and mindsets, B. Work ethics or submission to authority). If so, He may direct you to take that particular Day of the Scripture guide (e.g., Day Five) and include it with your daily speaking of Scriptures (i.e., Day One, Day Two, Day Three, and Day Four). What's important is to follow His leading. He knows what's best for you.

It would also be beneficial for you to (1) look up and read the Scripture references in *Heart-to-heart*, as this will help solidify the Lord's truth within you, and (2) take one portion of Scripture [e.g., 1(a), 1(b), 1(c), 1(d), 1(e)] and study, ponder, and pray over the corresponding study notes and Scriptures in the ***Scripture Guide Study Notes - Volume 2***. After this season is over, use the Scripture guide as needed.

When speaking aloud these Scriptures, there may be portions of Scripture where you desire more clarity or insight. When this occurs, go to the corresponding study notes in the ***Scripture Guide Study Notes - Volume 2***. If you still need further clarity, ask the Lord to help bring insight and clarity to you. There may be times when certain portions of Scripture may move you to tears or touch your heart deeply. When this occurs, you may find it beneficial to allow the Lord to minister to you as you sit quietly before Him. You also may need to pray further into this area. On the other hand, there may be times when speaking aloud these Scriptures that you may not feel engaged at all. If this occurs, I want to encourage you <u>to not give up</u>, but to continue as the Lord <u>originally</u> directed you. It is important to understand that regardless of how you feel, God's Word is at work within you, providing strength and growth to your inner man (Hebrews 4:12-14). Remember, this spiritual exercise is designed to help form new patterns of thinking in order for the born-again creation, the new man, to become a reality in your life.

> *But refuse profane and old wives' fables, and <u>exercise</u> thyself rather unto godliness. For bodily exercise profiteth little: but godliness is profitable unto all things, having promise of the life that now is, and of that which is to come.*
>
> (1 Timothy 4:7-8)

The Greek word for "exercise" is *gymnazo*. Its meaning in the Thayer's Greek Lexicon is "to exercise vigorously, in any way, either the body or the mind: of one who strives earnestly to become godly." Through this process, you are allowing the Word of God to work at a heart level within you and the end result will be victory over the old man and freedom in Christ as you go from faith to faith and glory to glory!

Also, when our hearts have become hardened through living out of the old man, as we soak in the Word of God by speaking aloud these Scriptures along with the "words of wisdom" from the Lord (*Heart-to-heart*) on a regular basis, His Word begins to soften any hardness of heart within us. This can be compared to immersing a baking dish with hardened residue into hot soapy water for a period of time in order for the residue to be easily removed and the baking dish cleaned (Malachi 3:2-3; Luke 8:15-17; Ephesians 5:25-27; Psalm 119:1-3, 9, 11, 13).

During this season, you may feel the need to reach out to a mature Christian or a Christian counselor who can help you walk through any areas of difficulty. Confessing your faults to another, after having confessed them to the Lord, will help you overcome as you bring them to the light and receive prayer, as well as healing (James 5:16) – for an example, please read **A Testimony**, Exhibit D. You may also find it beneficial to attend a healing ministry such as a *Living Waters Program* in order to bring you into an environment for the Lord to heal any wounding or bring to light any strongholds or root issues (e.g., carnal core beliefs and mindsets about yourself and others that formed and/or wounding that occurred during your formative years that keeps you bound to the old man). See **Support and Help**.

Although journaling is optional, I have included a ***Personal Prayer Journal – From your heart to His*** in order to help put off the old man by being honest with the Lord about things (e.g., fears and insecurities, cares and concerns, shortcomings and faults, anger and frustration). As Jesus was made to be sin for us, He, in turn, owns our sin and all that is associated with it, and He desires for us to release it to Him. Journaling to the Lord is prompted throughout the ***Personalized Scripture Guide***. For more detailed information on the importance of journaling, please refer to the ***Personal Prayer Journal – Details and Instructions***, Chapter 5.

Directive Two
Use ***Character Development in Christ*** as a study guide. Take one portion of Scripture [e.g., 1(a), (b), (c), (d), (e)] each week along with the corresponding "words of wisdom" from the Lord (*Heart-to-heart*) and study, ponder, and pray over the corresponding study notes and Scriptures in the ***Scripture Guide Study Notes - Volume 2***. It would also be beneficial for you to look up and read the Scripture references in *Heart-to-heart*, as this will help solidify the Lord's truth within you. You may, on occasion and/or during difficult times in your life, find it beneficial to speak aloud the personalized Scriptures, as outlined in Directive One, for two or three weeks or as needed. This will help you keep a fresh spiritual and mental attitude as it relates to the new man within you and your heavenly Father's steadfast love, care, and faithfulness toward you.

Directive Three
Use ***Character Development in Christ*** as reference material by using this ***Personalized Scripture Guide*** along with the Contents page and indexes in the ***Scripture Guide Study Notes - Volume 2***. You may, on occasion and/or during difficult times in your life, find it beneficial to speak aloud the personalized Scriptures, as outlined in Directive One, for two or three weeks or as needed. This will help you keep a fresh spiritual and mental attitude as it relates to the new man within you and your heavenly Father's steadfast love, care, and faithfulness toward you.

After prayerfully reading over these three directives, if you are not sure what the Lord would have you to do, I want to encourage you to just follow your heart. You may need to take the first step and then He will direct you. He always honors our pursuit of Christlikeness.

To Christian counselors and/or mature Christians who are discipling babes in Christ and/or helping those who are having difficulty overcoming aspects of the old man in their lives, I recommend that you prayerfully consider the following: Between meeting times, have them speak aloud the personalized Scriptures as outlined in Directive One, as a spiritual exercise, along with journaling their hearts to the Lord. This will allow His Word to bring to the surface anything that may be hidden. During your next meeting, encourage them to share anything the Lord has revealed in order to release more of the old man and to receive healing prayer and encouragement. For an example, please refer to ***A Testimony***, Exhibit D.

IMPORTANT NOTICE

As a reminder, this Scripture guide is not intended to be used as a legalistic religious activity, but a vehicle to help you renew the *spirit of your mind* or your *inmost mind*, and to nourish and strengthen your inner man. I want to encourage you to not be overwhelmed or pressured into thinking you have to complete each day as this guide suggests. As you begin speaking aloud the personalized Scriptures along with the *Heart-to-heart*, allow the Lord to direct you. For example, during Day One, you may be touched by a portion of Scripture or a "word of wisdom" from the Lord (*Heart-to-heart*). You may feel you want to pray or meditate further into this area during the remainder of your time with Him. If this occurs, please do so. The next day, pick up where you left off.

On the other hand, as you spend time familiarizing yourself with the guide and using it for a few weeks, you may find, for example: (1) you would like to speak aloud Day One and Day Two in one sitting, or (2) as in Lisa's case, where she so graciously shared in the last paragraph of her testimony (Exhibit D), the Lord may show you that you need to concentrate on certain portions of Scripture throughout the week where your inner man needs more reinforcement or strength (e.g., Part Three – A. Behavior patterns and mindsets, B. Work ethics or submission to authority). If so, He may direct you to take that particular Day of the Scripture guide (e.g., Day Five) and include it with your daily speaking of Scriptures (i.e., Day One, Day Two, Day Three, and Day Four). What's important is to follow His leading. He knows what's best for you.

SCRIPTURE GUIDE - PART ONE

SCRIPTURES DESIGNED TO HELP PUT OFF THE OLD MAN CONCERNING:

- **Cares and Anxieties of this World and Distractions of the Age (thorn plants that choke the Word and It becomes unfruitful)**

Along with corresponding
words of wisdom from the Lord

-Heart-to-heart-

"Other seed [of the same kind] fell among thorn plants, and the thistles grew and pressed together and utterly choked and suffocated it, and it yielded no grain." Mark 4:7 (AMPCE)

"And the ones sown among the thorns are others who hear the Word; Then the cares and anxieties of the world and distractions of the age, and the pleasure and delight and false glamour and deceitfulness of riches, and the craving and passionate desire for other things creep in and choke and suffocate the Word, and it becomes fruitless." Mark 4:18-19 (AMPCE)

"Likewise, ye younger, submit yourselves unto the elder. Yea, all of you be subject one to another, and be clothed with humility: for God resisteth the proud, and giveth grace to the humble. Humble yourselves therefore under the mighty hand of God, that he may exalt you in due time: casting all your care upon him; for he careth for you. Be sober, be vigilant; because your adversary the devil, as a roaring lion, walketh about, seeking whom he may devour: whom resist stedfast in the faith, knowing that the same afflictions are accomplished in your brethren that are in the world." 1 Peter 5:5-9

"And let the peace of God rule in your hearts, to the which also ye are called in one body; and be ye thankful." Colossians 3:15

Day One
1(a) *You are **Elohim – the Creator God.*** **(b)** *You are my God. You made me and You made my world.* **(c)** *Thank You for all that You have given me.* **(d)** How precious and weighty also are Your thoughts to me, O God! How vast is the sum of them! If I could count them, they would be more in number than the sand. **(e)** …[And the Lord answered] Can a woman forget her nursing child, that she should not have compassion on the son of her womb? Yes, they may forget, yet I will not forget you. (Psalm 118:28-AMPCE; Psalm 139:17-18-AMPCE; Isaiah 49:14-15-AMPCE.) (Ref.: Genesis 1:1; Romans 8; Psalm 139:14-16; Ephesians 5:20; 1 Thessalonians 5:18; Hebrews 13:15.)

Heart-to-heart
Do not allow your worth and value to be determined by what man, including yourself, thinks or says about you. Your worth and value comes from Me—your Creator. Renew your mind to My truths where you will begin to comprehend the vastness of My love for you and find abundant life. My love runs much deeper than your imperfections, failures, and insecurities. Rest in Me and know that you bring pleasure to My heart when you give thanks. I will never forget you. I am your Father, I am your strength, and I am in touch with every detail of your life, so fear not! Open your heart to Me and allow Me to come in and bring nourishment to you, for I am the only One who is able to fulfill the deep longings of your heart. (Ref.: Psalm 56:11, 118:6; Hebrews 13:5-6. Psalm 139:1-18; Romans 8:16-39. Romans 12:1-2; Ephesians 4:21-24, 3:14-21; John 10:10. Ephesians 3:14-21; Psalm 139:17-18. Romans 8:35-39; 1 Thessalonians 5:18. Isaiah 49:15. Romans 8:15-17; Psalm 18:2, 27:1; 2 Samuel 22:33; Matthew 10:29-31. Revelation 3:20; 1 Peter 2:2-3; John 6:48-51, 1:1-3, 14; John 4:6-18; John 7:37-39.)

2(a) *You are **El-Olam – the Everlasting One.*** **(b)** Your kingdom is an everlasting kingdom, and Your dominion endures throughout all generations. (Psalm 145:13-AMPCE.) (Ref.: Genesis 21:33.)

Heart-to-heart
All power and authority is Mine—I am the King of kings and the Lord of lords and I rule with truth, justice, and mercy. Compared to eternity, your life on this earth is as a vapor. Walk in My ways and know that in Me you live and move and have your being. Fear not for it is your Father's good pleasure to give you the kingdom: righteousness, peace, and joy in the Holy Spirit. I desire to have fellowship with you and to reveal Myself to you. Receive Me as Lord and you will have everlasting life. (Ref.: 1 Corinthians

1:23-24; Matthew 28:18; 1 Timothy 6:14-16; Psalm 89:14. James 4:14. Isaiah 55:7-13; Luke 6:46-49; Acts 17:28. Luke 12:31-32; 2 Peter 1:1-11; Romans 14:17. John 14:23-24; Matthew 16:13-18. John 3:16; Romans 10:9.)

3(a) *You are* **Alpha and Omega, the beginning and the ending, the first and the last, the Almighty.** *There* is no God in heaven above or on earth below like You. **(b)** *You are* the author and finisher of *my* faith. (Revelations 1:8, 11; 1 Kings 8:23-NKJV; Hebrews 12:2.)

♡ *Heart-to-heart*
Your mind is not able to comprehend the vastness of who I am. I have designed the inner workings of your spirit to be able to connect with Me on a deeper level than mere intellect can obtain. Through this connection, faith is conceived and nurtured to enable you to receive from Me the plan and purpose that I have for you. Do not be deceived in thinking that your way is the right way; there is a way that seems right to a man but the end is death. I am the way, the truth, and the life; therefore, follow Me and live by faith to obtain true victory. Broad is the way to destruction, but strait and narrow is the way which leads to life; choose life that you and your seed may live. (Ref.: Isaiah 40:28-31; 55:8-9; Romans 11:33-36; Ephesians 3:14-21. 1 Corinthians 2:9-16; John 3:5-6, 6:63, 4:24; Romans 12:1-2; Ephesians 4:20-24. Romans 10:17; Hebrews 11:1; Romans 11:29; Ephesians 2:10. Mark 8:34-38; Galatians 6:7-8; Proverbs 14:12. John 14:6; Mark 8:34-38; 1 John 5:4. Matthew 7:13-14; Deuteronomy 30:19.)

4(a) *You are* **Yahweh-Shammah – the LORD is there.** **(b)** Though I walk through the [deep, sunless] valley of the shadow of death, I will fear or dread no evil, for You are with me. (Psalm 23:4-AMPCE.) *(Ref.: Ezekiel 48:35.)*

♡ *Heart-to-heart*
I am Omnipotent—all ruling and Almighty; so fear not in times of trouble for I am with you in it and through it. My love for you is everlasting and there is nothing that can separate you from My love. Trust Me in all things. (Ref.: Revelation 19:6, 15:3; John 8:56-58; Exodus 3:13-14; Psalm 9:9-10, 34:17; Isaiah 43:11-14; Psalm 23. Ephesians 3:14-21; Romans 8:31-39. Psalm 36:7, 18:2; Isaiah 12:2; 1 Peter 2:24-25; Matthew 11:28-30, 28:18; Hebrews 6:17-20; Romans 8:31-39.)

5(a) *You are* **the Light of the world. (b)** *You are* my light and my salvation; whom *(or what)* shall I fear? The entrance of *Your* words *gives* light; it *gives* understanding to the simple. Your word is a lamp to my feet and a light to my path. Show me Your ways, O LORD; teach me Your paths. Lead me in Your truth and teach me, for You are the God of my salvation; on You I wait all the day. **(c)** *You* lead the humble in what is right and the humble *You teach Your ways*. *I* clothe *myself* with humility [as the garb of a servant, so that its covering cannot possibly be stripped from *me*, with freedom from pride and arrogance] toward *others*. For *You set Yourself* against the proud, but *You give grace* to the humble. *As I walk in humility, lowliness of mind and trusting in You, my* life shall be clearer than the noonday and rise above *my misery*; though there be darkness, it shall be as the morning. Light is sown for *me* and strewn along *my* pathway, and joy [the irrepressible joy which comes from consciousness of *Your* favor and protection]. **(d)** All the days of the desponding and afflicted are made evil [by anxious thoughts and forebodings], <u>but he who has a glad heart has a continual feast [regardless of circumstances]</u>. (John 8:12-AMPCE; Psalm 27:1, 119:130, 105-NKJV, 25:4-5-NKJV, 25:9-AMPCE; 1 Peter 5:5-AMPCE; Job 11:17-AMPCE; Psalm 97:11-AMPCE; Proverbs 15:15-AMPCE.) *(Ref.: Romans 8:31-39; Philippians 2:3-13.)*

<u>Heart-to-heart</u>

I am the true Light and I have come to dispel darkness within you—to destroy the works of the devil. The entrance of My Word brings light to your very being—as if someone entered into a dark room and turned on the light switch; so too My Words bring forth understanding to your mind in order for you to see how to walk in this life according to My will. Stay focused on Me for I have come to give you life and that more abundantly. Humble yourself and submit to Me that it may go well with you, for all of My paths are mercy and truth. (Ref.: John 1:6-18, 8:12; 1 John 3:8. Psalm 119:130; John 17:17; Ephesians 4:18-24; 1 Peter 2:9-11; 2 Peter 1:19-21. Luke 11:33-36; Colossians 3:1-4; John 10:10-11. 1 Peter 5:5-11; Deuteronomy 12:28; Psalm 25:10.)

6(a) *You are* **LORD** – *You are* **a man of war. (b)** The name of the LORD *is* a strong tower: *I run into it and I am safe. You are* my hiding place and my shield; I hope in Your word. *You preserve me from trouble and surround me with songs of deliverance. You* only *are* my rock and my salvation; *You are* my defense; I shall not be moved. I LOVE You, fervently and devotedly, O Lord, my Strength. *You are my God* in Whom I will trust and take refuge. If God be for *me*, who *or what* can be against *me*? *You are* on my side; I will not fear: what can man do *to* me? (Exodus 15:3; Proverbs 18:10;

Psalm 119:114, 62:6, 18:1-2-AMPCE; Romans 8:31; Psalm 118:6-NKJV.) *(Ref.: Psalm 32:7; Romans 8:31-39.)*

♡♡ Heart-to-heart

Many of My children have their own protective coverings to ward off pain due to rejection, abandonment, and insecurities in order to protect themselves from a hurting world and in turn hurting others with a defensive posture and a sharp tongue. This behavior comes from bitterness, resentment, and unforgiveness. I am a man of war and I alone desire to be your protective covering through My shed blood. I have come to set you free from your pain and insecurities, and to remove the false covering that surrounds your heart. Trust Me and allow Me to bring healing to you; I am the Shepherd and Bishop of your soul. (Ref.: 2 Corinthians 10:3-6; Romans 8:1-8; 1 Corinthians 3:1-3; Ephesians 4:31-32. Hebrews 12:14-17; Matthew 6:14-15. Exodus 15:3; Ephesians 1:1-12. Isaiah 53:5-6; Hebrews 4:12-16; 2 Corinthians 10:3-6; Romans 2:28-29; Colossians 2:10-11. Psalm 23, 36:7; John 10:11, 16:33; 1 Peter 2:24-25.)

7(a) You are **Abba, Father**. I thank You that I have received Your precious Holy Spirit which <u>produces sonship</u> making You my Father. **(b)** I can trust that You have my best interest at heart! **(c)** Just as Jesus cried out to You in the hour of temptation, "Abba, [which means] Father, everything is possible for You. Take away this cup from Me; yet not what I will, but what You [will]." *I too trust my life to You today, not my will but Your will be done.* (Mark 14:36-AMPCE.) *(Ref.: Romans 8:15-AMPCE; Galatians 4:6-7; Jeremiah 29:11, 32:38-41; Hebrews 12:5-11; Mark 14:35; 1 Peter 2:21-23.)*

♡♡ Heart-to-heart

Through My Son's humble obedience to death on the cross, many sons and daughters have been birthed into My kingdom. My love and faithfulness to you, My child, passes knowledge and I have your best interest at heart! In Jesus' darkest hour He chose to trust Me and My plan and purpose for Him while on the earth; the pain and suffering He endured was My will because of My great love for you. Because of His obedience, I have given Him a name above every name and at that name every knee shall bow and every tongue shall confess that He is Lord; all power has been given to Him both in heaven and in earth. I desire for all of My sons and daughters to be obedient to Me and to trust Me, as Jesus did, even in their darkest hour. The key to fulfilling My plan and purpose for your life is through prayer and renewing your mind to My truths, receiving My strength to resist temptation and to walk in trusting obedience. I love you! (Ref.: Philippians 2:8-11; John 3:1-8; 1 Peter 1:18-25, 2:2-3; Galatians 4:1-7; Romans 8:11-18. Ephesians

3:14-21; Psalm 36:5, 139:15-18; Deuteronomy 6:24-25; Jeremiah 32:38-41; Hebrews 12:9-11; Romans 8:28-39. Mark 14:33-42; Matthew 27:45-46; Hebrews 5:7-10; John 3:14-17. Philippians 2:8-11; Romans 14:10-12; Matthew 28:18-20. Hebrews 5:7-10; 1 Peter 2:18-25; Psalm 23. Mark 14:37-38; Romans 12:1-2; Ephesians 4:20-24; James 1:12-18; Hebrews 5:7-10. John 3:16-17; 1 John 4:19.)

8(a) *You are* **Yahweh-Shalom – The Prince of Peace.** **(b)** The government shall be upon *Your* shoulder: and *Your name* shall be called Wonderful, Counsellor, The mighty God, The everlasting Father, The Prince of Peace. **(c)** *Jesus, You said,* "In the world you have tribulation and trials and distress and frustration; but be of good cheer [take courage; be confident, certain, undaunted]! For I have overcome the world. [I have deprived it of power to harm you and have conquered it for you.] **(d)** Peace I leave with you; My [own] peace I now give and bequeath to you. Not as the world gives do I give to you. Do not let your *heart* be troubled, neither let *it* be afraid. [Stop allowing *yourself* to be agitated and disturbed; and do not permit *yourself* to be fearful and intimidated and cowardly and unsettled.]" (Isaiah 9:6; John 16:33-AMPCE, 14:27-AMPCE.) *(Ref.: Isaiah 9:6.)*

♥♥ *Heart-to-heart*

I am calling you to abide in Me, in My life and peace, as you were not created to live apart from Me. I died so that My Spirit could dwell within you and you could be one with Me, as I desire to be one with you. I have overcome the world, I have destroyed the works of the devil, and I'm calling you to partake in My finished work. Do not be consumed with this world, being fretful and full of fear and anger. I have not called you to trust in your feelings and emotions, I have called you to trust in My truth and My love for you! Release your fears to Me, release your anger to Me, release your cares to Me, for I care for you. (Ref.: John 15:1-11, 1:1-4, 14. Romans 8:1-11; Galatians 4:6; John 17:17-24. John 16:33; 1 John 3:8; John 17:4, 19:30; 2 Peter 1:1-11. Mark 4:11-20; 1 John 2:15-17; Matthew 24:35. 2 Corinthians 4:6-18; John 8:31-36; Romans 8:31-39. John 14:27-AMPCE; Psalm 62:5-8, 142:2; 1 Peter 5:6-11, 2:21-25.)

---

9. So, Lord, I respond to You right now by giving You all of **my cares**, **my concerns**, and **my fears** which include situations and circumstances that have caused me to **feel anxious, worried, depressed, hurt, disappointed, insecure, intimidated,** or **threatened** because You care for me. I also give You the things that **agitate, anger, disturb,** or **frustrate** me, and **the things that I am unsettled with.** *I realize that these thoughts* *and feelings are the very things that keep me from living in Your peace and operating in clarity of mind and heart, so I choose to be specific as I pour out my heart to You. (Ref.: Psalm 62:8, 142:2; 1 Peter 5:5-7; John 14:27.)*

🛑 If you are dealing with any of these feelings or emotions, it is important to release them to your heavenly Father, otherwise they can hold you captive to the old man and can also build within and like a volcano erupt onto others. Please refer to Chapter 5, ***Personal Prayer Journal – From your heart to His,*** **designed to help put off the old man. Part One encourages you to cast your cares, concerns, and/or fears upon your heavenly Father because He cares for you. Part Three encourages you to be real (honest) with Him concerning issues of the heart, listed in 9, which hinder you from living out of the new man. If you need to journal your heart to the Lord concerning any cares, concerns, and/or fears, you may not have the time right now. I want to encourage you when things arise, release them to Him. This is here to remind you of the importance of being real (honest) with the Lord. So, if you do not have anything to give to Him or do not have the time now, please continue…**

10(a) *I let the peace (soul harmony which comes) from Christ rule (act as umpire continually) in my heart [deciding and settling with finality all questions that arise in my mind, in that peaceful state] to which as a [member of Christ's] one body I have been called [to live].* **(b)** *I am thankful (appreciative), [giving praise to You always] – making melody to You with [Your] grace in my heart.* (Colossians 3:15-16-AMPCE.)

💕 *<u>Heart-to-heart</u>*
I have a plan and a purpose for your life, therefore, humble yourself before Me in complete surrender to the One who formed you in your mother's womb. The thief comes to steal from you through carnal behavior: lust, pride, unforgiveness, ungodly thoughts, and half-truths that would try to pull you away from Me and My will for your life. I desire to lead you to a good land, to conquer your enemies within you, and to give you abundant life just as I did for the children of Israel back in the days of Moses and Joshua. But I cannot force you to trust Me and surrender your will to Mine, just as I could not force the children of Israel. Forty years passed before they entered the land that I promised them because of their own fears and unbelief. Trust Me and let My love cast out your fears and My peace rule in your heart. I am the Lord and I change not. (Ref.: Ephesians 2:4-10; Romans 8:29, 12:1-2; James 4:6-8; 1 Peter 5:5-10; Psalm 139:13-18. John 10:10; Ephesians 2:1-10; Genesis 3:1-19; 2 Corinthians 10:3-6; Ephesians 6:10-18.

Luke 17:20-21; 1 John 3:8; John 10:10; Deuteronomy 8:1-18. Philippians 2:12-13; Numbers 14:1-21. Numbers 14:22-45; Joshua 1:1-9. Colossians 3:1-4; Hebrews 12:1-2; 1 John 4:18; John 14:27, 16:33; Colossians 3:15. Malachi 3:6; Hebrews 13:8.)

---

11. *I understand that* whatsoever is born of God *overcomes* the world: and this is the victory that *overcomes* the world, even *my* faith. (1 John 5:4.)

<u>*Heart-to-heart*</u>
Faith comes from the heart through hearing My Word: it is impossible to please Me without it and all things are possible with it. Many of My children start out with faith and give up without receiving a promise from Me and become discouraged because patience was not present to endure the pressures and trials of this life: for it is through faith and patience that you inherit the promises. The trying of your faith works patience within you, and as you allow patience to have her perfect work, you will be complete and whole wanting nothing. I have called you to be an overcomer in this life, to be victorious—to walk in righteousness, peace, and joy in the midst of uncertainty, disappointments, fears, and so-called failures, which when operating in faith can become pearls of wisdom. Turn from your doubt and unbelief and feed on My Words and drink in My Spirit through praise and thanksgiving, then faith will begin to come forth within you. Do not be moved by your circumstances, your feelings, or your emotions but stay the course of faith. Release your fears and concerns to Me for I am here to receive them and to give you new life. (Ref.: Romans 10:8-17; John 6:63; John 15:7; Hebrews 11:6; Mark 9:23. Luke 8:11-15; Hebrews 6:12-20. James 1:3-4. 1 John 5:4-5; Romans 14:17; 1 Corinthians 4:20; Acts 20:32, 14:22; 2 Corinthians 4:6-18; Romans 8:36-39; 1 Corinthians 1:23-24. Mark 16:14; Romans 11:20-23; Romans 10:10-17; 1 Peter 2:2; John 7:37-39; Psalm 100:1-5; Ephesians 5:15-20. 2 Corinthians 4:16-18; John 14:27-AMPCE. Psalm 62:8, 142:2; 1 Peter 5:5-7; John 10:10; Romans 6:4-6.)

---

12. *I thank You, Lord, that* all authority (all power of rule) in heaven and on earth has been given to *You. You have destroyed* the works of the devil, *and I am in You and You are in me. I thank You for Your faithfulness in my life. I choose to look* away [from all that will distract] to, *You,* Jesus. *My focus is on You today!* (Matthew 28:18-AMPCE; 1 John 3:8; Hebrews 12:2-AMPCE.) (Ref.: Hebrews 2:11; Acts 17:28; 1 Peter 4:19; Hebrews 12:2.)

♡ Heart-to-heart

Be wise! Set your affections on things above where I abide. For in Me there is abundant life—fullness of righteousness, peace, and joy. There is a life-giving flow of My Spirit within those who choose to stay focused on Me and trust Me even in the midst of trials and hardships. Let your hope and expectation be in Me. (Ref.: Proverbs 23:19-21; James 3:13-18; Daniel 12:2-3. Colossians 3:1-4. John 10:10; Romans 14:17. John 7:37-39, 16:33; Acts 14:22; Psalm 23; Hebrews 12:1-2. Romans 12:12, 15:13; Philippians 1:20-30.)

- I choose to stay focused on You during my day-to-day life. (Ref.: Hebrews 12:1-2.)
- I choose to take one day at a time – not to focus on next week or next month, but to receive Your grace today and to enjoy what You have given me today. (Ref.: Matthew 6:24-34; 2 Corinthians 12:9.)
- I choose to hold fast, in my mind and heart, the Words of life. (Ref.: Proverbs 4:20-23.)
- I choose to let Your Words become more real to me than what I see, what I hear, and ultimately, what I think and feel. (Ref.: 2 Corinthians 4:17-18.)
- I choose to allow You to take me deeper in Your love, understanding this requires death to the old man, the false self. (Ref.: Ephesians 3:16-21, 4:20-24.)
- I choose to live by faith and not by sight, to live out of my spirit, my new nature, and not out of my flesh, my carnal nature: to be eternally minded and not temporal minded. For the things which are seen are temporary but the things which are not seen are eternal —deathless and everlasting. (Ref.: Habakkuk 2:4; Galatians 3:11; Romans 1:17, 8:29, 12:1-2; 1 Corinthians 15:45-49; 2 Corinthians 4:18-AMPCE.)
- I choose to trust You in every situation and circumstance of life. (Ref.: 1 Peter 2:21-25.)

I want to encourage you to pray this to Him, "*Lord, let Your Words of truth penetrate my heart and my soul, dismantling the carnality within me, and bring forth the new man.*" Now, I want to encourage you to be quiet before the Lord for a few minutes communing with Him without spoken words.

Note:
- Where the word of a king is, there is power (Ecclesiastes 8:4; 1 Timothy 6:12-16).
- For the word of God is living and powerful, and sharper than any two-edged sword, piercing even to the division of soul and spirit, and of joints and marrow, and is a discerner of the thoughts and intents of the heart (Hebrews 4:12-NKJV).

SCRIPTURE GUIDE - PART TWO

SCRIPTURES DESIGNED TO HELP PUT OFF THE OLD MAN CONCERNING:

- **False Glamour, Deceitfulness of Riches, and the Craving and Passionate Desire for Other Things (thorn plants that choke the Word and It becomes unfruitful)**

Along with corresponding words of wisdom from the Lord

Heart-to-heart

"Other seed [of the same kind] fell among thorn plants, and the thistles grew and pressed together and utterly choked and suffocated it, and it yielded no grain." Mark 4:7 (AMPCE)

"And the ones sown among the thorns are others who hear the Word; Then the cares and anxieties of the world and distractions of the age, and the pleasure and delight and false glamour and deceitfulness of riches, and the craving and passionate desire for other things creep in and choke and suffocate the Word, and it becomes fruitless." Mark 4:18-19 (AMPCE)

"The night is far spent, the day is at hand: let us therefore cast off the works of darkness, and let us put on the armour of light. Let us walk honestly, as in the day; not in rioting and drunkenness, not in chambering and wantonness, not in strife and envying. But put ye on the Lord Jesus Christ, and make not provision for the flesh, to fulfil the lusts thereof." Romans 13:12-14

"Mortify therefore your members which are upon the earth; fornication, uncleanness, inordinate affection, evil concupiscence, and covetousness, which is idolatry: For which things' sake the wrath of God cometh on the children of disobedience:" Colossians 3:5-6.

Day Two

13(a) *You are **Yeshua**, my salvation. You sent Moses to deliver Israel from Egypt, You raised up judges to deliver Israel from their enemies, and You've sent Jesus to deliver me from my sin.* **(b)** *Continue to lead the way, Lord, and I will follow You to the promised land, the kingdom of God that dwells within my heart! (Ref.: Exodus 15:2; Exodus 3:1-10; Judges 2:16; John 1:29; Luke 17:21, 6:46-49.)*

♡ *Heart-to-heart*
My kingdom is an everlasting kingdom and My dominion endures throughout all generations. All power has been given to Me both in heaven and in earth and I am with you to free you from the law of sin and death. I became sin when I was nailed to the cross, a sacrifice to God as a sweet-smelling fragrance. If I gave Myself for you, how much more by Me, will your heavenly Father freely give you all things that pertain to life and godliness. If God be for you who can be against you; trust Me in all things, for I am with you to deliver you from this present evil time: to sit with Me in heavenly places. (Ref.: Psalm 145:13; Daniel 4:3, 7:27; 2 Peter 1:1-11. Matthew 28:18; Romans 8:1-6; Hebrews 2:14-15. 2 Corinthians 5:20-21; Ephesians 5:1-2. Romans 8:32-39; 2 Peter 1:1-4. Romans 8:28-39; 1 Timothy 4:10; Galatians 1:3-5; Ephesians 2:5-7; Psalm 27:1-6.)

14(a) *You are **Adonai – Lord.*** **(b)** *You are my Lord; I have no good beside or beyond You. (Psalm 16:2-AMPCE.) (Ref.: Psalm 16:2.)*

♡ *Heart-to-heart*
While My Son walked this earth, He knew there was no good thing in His flesh to draw from as He understood that all goodness comes from Me. Neither did He say or do anything apart from Me and trusted Me even to His death. My Spirit empowers you to walk in complete trust in Me as you grow in grace and knowledge through My Words and in fellowship with one another. I have given you the mind of Christ and I have predestined you to be conformed to His image. Eye has not seen, nor ear heard, nor have entered into the heart of man, the things which I have prepared for those who love Me. But I have revealed them to those by My Spirit: for My Spirit searches all things, yes, the deep treasures of My heart. I have much to offer to the ones who seek Me with their whole heart and are obedient to Me. (Ref.: Matthew 19:16-17; Psalm 31:19, 33:5; Ephesians 5:8-10; 2 Thessalonians 1:11-12. John 12:49-50, 3:34-36, 8:28-30, 5:19-24, 14:10-12; Luke 22:41-44. 2 Corinthians 3:17-18; Acts 20:32; 2 Peter 3:18; 1 John 1:7. 1 Corinthians 2:16; Romans 8:29. 1 Corinthians 2:9; John 14:21-24. 1 Corinthians 2:10; Colossians 2:1-3. Psalm 119:2; Lamentations 3:22-25; 1 Peter 1:1-16.)

15(a) *You are **Qanna – Jealous**.* For *I will* worship no other god: for the LORD, whose name *is* Jealous, *is* a jealous God. **(b)** *I choose to* keep *myself* from idols (false gods)–[from anything and everything that would occupy the place in *my* heart due to *You*, from any sort of substitute for *You* that would take first place in *my* life]. *Help me to see and remove anything in my heart that is taking Your rightful place as my God.* (Exodus 34:14; 1 John 5:21-AMPCE.) *(Ref.: Exodus 34:14; Hebrews 4:12-13; Philippians 2:12-13.)*

♡ *Heart-to-heart*
My love for you is as immeasurable as the grains of sand on all the seashores in all the world. There is no one on this earth that loves you or knows you as I do and I desire intimacy with you. I desire that you know Me, and as you seek to know Me you will find all that you are looking for. When you choose to go after My creation and lustful acts to try to satisfy the deep longings of your heart, instead of Me—your Creator, you will continue to stay thirsty and empty. Only I can satisfy the deep cries of your heart and soul to where you will never thirst again; I am the fountain of living waters that springs up within you into everlasting life. Idolatry stops the life flow of My Spirit and grieves My heart. (Ref.: Ephesians 3:14-21; Psalm 139:17-18. John 3:16-21; Psalm 139:1-3; Revelation 3:20-22; John 14:21-23. John 17:3; Psalm 37:4; 2 Peter 1:2-4. 1 John 2:15-17; John 4:3-18. John 7:37-39; Jeremiah 17:13. Luke 12:15-31; Colossians 3:1-6; 1 Corinthians 10:1-14; Ephesians 4:30.)

16(a) *You are **Yahweh-Sabaoth – the LORD of Hosts**. Hosts in Hebrew means a mass of persons organized for war.* O LORD God of hosts, who *is* mighty like You? **(b)** Your faithfulness also surrounds You. *I trust Your might and Your faithfulness in my life to free me from all things that keep me from being like You.* (Psalm 89:8-NKJV.) *(Ref.: Psalm 46:11; Hebrews 4:12-13; Philippians 2:12-13; Romans 8:29-30.)*

♡ *Heart-to-heart*
The baptism of My Holy Spirit is My gift and promise to you. He is the same Spirit that brought creation into existence. He is the same Spirit that descended upon Jesus when He was baptized. He is the same Spirit that raised Christ from the dead. Through My Spirit within My Son, many miracles took place and even as the apostle John wrote, "There are also many other things which Jesus did, the which, if they should be written every one, I suppose that even the world itself could not contain the books that should be written." As you surrender your life to Me, My Spirit and the Word of My power will set you free from sin and conform you into the image of My dear Son. By My Spirit, My love

has been poured out in your heart to free you from your fears and demonic strongholds that wage war against your soul. (Ref.: John 7:37-39; Acts 11:13-17, 2:38-39. Genesis 1:1-31. Luke 3:21-22. Romans 8:11. John 11:47, 21:25. Acts 1:5-8; Hebrews 1:1-6, 4:12-16; John 8:31-36; 2 Corinthians 3:17-18; Romans 8:29. Romans 5:5; 1 John 4:18; 2 Corinthians 10:3-6.)

17(a) If then *I* have been raised with Christ [to a new life, thus sharing His resurrection from the dead], *I* aim at and seek the [rich, eternal treasures] that are above, where Christ is, seated at the right hand of God. And <u>*I* set *my mind* and keep it set on what is above (the higher things), not on the things that are on the earth. For [as far as this world is concerned] *I* have died, and *my* [new, real] life is hidden with Christ in God. When Christ, Who is *my* life, appears, then *I* also will appear with Him in [the splendor of His] glory.</u> **(b)** *Therefore, I put off the old man by putting to death (depriving of power)* the evil desire lurking in my members [those animal impulses and all that is earthly in *me* that is employed in sin]: sexual vice, impurity, sensual appetites, unholy desires, and all greed and covetousness, for that is idolatry (the deifying of self and other created things instead of God). It is on account of these [very sins] that the [holy] anger of God is ever coming upon the sons of disobedience (those who are obstinately opposed to the divine will). (Colossians 3:1-6-AMPCE.)*(Ref.: Colossians 3:5, 9.)*

Heart-to-heart
I am the giver of your life and the length of your days, and through My sacrifice I have made it possible for you to live in Me and to experience My glory. Set your mind on the eternal riches of My glory; be captivated by your Creator who loves you and gave His life for you. Compared to eternity, your life on this earth is as a vapor, it appears a little time and vanishes away. Use your time wisely, choose life and follow after Me. (Ref.: Genesis 1:26-28; Psalm 139:13-16; Proverbs 3:1-2; Hebrews 10:1-27; Acts 17:28; John 1:1-3, 14; Colossians 1:27; 2 Corinthians 4:6-7. Colossians 3:1-4; 1 Peter 5:5-10; Romans 9:23-24, 11:33-36; John 3:16-17. James 4:14-15. Ephesians 5:14-17; 1 Peter 1:22-25; Matthew 16:24-26; John 8:31-36.)

If you need to repent of anything listed in 17b please go to Chapter 5, Part Two. It is important to release them to your heavenly Father through repentance. This behavior originates from the old man and must be put to death. If you need to journal your heart to the Lord concerning any of these carnal behaviors, you may not have the time right now. However, it

is important to take the time to repent of them. I want to encourage you, if any of these behaviors have become strongholds in your life, please be real with the Lord and ask Him for His help to overcome. This is here to remind you of the importance of being real (honest) with the Lord. So, if you do not have anything to give to Him or if you do not have the time now, please continue…

18(a) For if *I* live according to [the dictates of] the flesh, *I* will surely die. But if through the power of the [Holy] Spirit <u>*I am* [habitually] putting to death (making extinct, deadening) the [evil] deeds prompted by the body, *I* shall [really and genuinely] live forever</u>. For all who are led by the Spirit of God are sons of God. Search me, O God, and know my heart: try me, and know my thoughts: and see if *there be any* wicked way in me, and lead me in the way everlasting. **(b)** *For* the thief comes only in order to steal and kill and destroy. *You* came that *I* may have and enjoy life, and have it in abundance (to the full, till it overflows). (Romans 8:13-14-AMPCE; Psalm 139:23-24; John 10:10-AMPCE.)

Heart-to-heart
I have called you to a new life and My grace is within you to give you the ability to set your mind and affections on the eternal treasures that are in Christ. My law is holy; therefore, it is impossible for the carnal man to abide in it. Jesus fulfilled My will and bore carnality in His own body on the cross in order for you to become born again and walk in love, the fulfilling of the law. I have called you to be married to Christ and to bring forth fruit unto Me; for out of My Son's sacrifice a new covenant was made and the church was born! As you choose to yield yourself to My Son and His love for you, you will begin to experience the abundant life He died to give to you. Flee youthful lusts and follow after righteousness, faith, love, and peace with those who call upon Me out of a pure heart. (Ref.: Romans 6:1-4; Acts 20:32; 2 Peter 3:18; Colossians 3:1-6; 2 Corinthians 4:6-7. Romans 7. 1 Peter 2:24-25; John 3:1-8; 1 Peter 1:22-2:3; Ephesians 4:20-24; Romans 13:8-14; Colossians 3:5-14. Romans 7:4-6; Ephesians 5:23-32; Galatians 5:22-26; Hebrews 10:16-22; Acts 2. Ephesians 3:14-21; Colossians 2:1-7; John 10:10; 2 Peter 1:2-11. 2 Timothy 2:20-22.)

I want to encourage you to pray this to Him, "*Lord, let Your Words of truth penetrate my heart and my soul, dismantling the carnality within me, and bring forth the new man.*" Now, I want to encourage you to be quiet before the Lord for a few minutes communing with Him without spoken words.

Note:
- Where the word of a king is, there is power (Ecclesiastes 8:4; 1 Timothy 6:12-16).
- For the word of God is living and powerful, and sharper than any two-edged sword, piercing even to the division of soul and spirit, and of joints and marrow, and is a discerner of the thoughts and intents of the heart (Hebrews 4:12-NKJV).

SCRIPTURE GUIDE - PART THREE

SCRIPTURES DESIGNED TO HELP PUT OFF THE OLD MAN AND PUT ON THE NEW MAN CONCERNING:

A. Behavior Patterns and Mindsets

Along with corresponding words of wisdom from the Lord

-Heart-to-heart-

"The night is far spent, the day is at hand: let us therefore cast off the works of darkness, and let us put on the armour of light. Let us walk honestly, as in the day; not in rioting and drunkenness, not in chambering and wantonness, not in strife and envying. But put ye on the Lord Jesus Christ, and make not provision for the flesh, to fulfil the lusts thereof." Romans 13:12-14

"For as many of you as have been baptized into Christ have put on Christ. There is neither Jew nor Greek, there is neither bond nor free, there is neither male nor female: for ye are all one in Christ Jesus. And if ye be Christ's, then are ye Abraham's seed, and heirs according to the promise." Galatians 3:27-29

"That ye put off concerning the former conversation (behavior) the old man, which is corrupt according to the deceitful lusts; And be renewed in the spirit of your mind; and that ye put on the new man, which after God is created in righteousness and true holiness." Ephesians 4:22-24

"But now ye also put off all these; anger, wrath, malice, blasphemy, filthy communication out of your mouth. Lie not one to another, seeing that ye have put off the old man with his deeds; and have put on the new man, which is renewed in knowledge after the image of him that created him: where there is neither Greek nor Jew, circumcision nor uncircumcision, Barbarian, Scythian, bond nor free: but Christ is all, and in all. Put on therefore, as the elect of God, holy and beloved, bowels of mercies, kindness, humbleness of mind, meekness, longsuffering; Forbearing one another, and forgiving one another, if any man have a quarrel against any: even as Christ forgave you, so also do ye. And above all these things put on charity (God's love), which is the bond of perfectness." Colossians 3:8-14

Day Three

19(a) *You are **Yahweh – LORD**. I understand that You are the LORD. Before You there was no God formed, neither shall there be after You.* **(b)** *Besides You there is no savior. (Ref.: Isaiah 43:10-11.)*

Heart-to-heart
Be still, and know that I am God: I will be exalted among the nations, I will be exalted in the earth. (Ref.: Psalm 46:10.)

20(a) *You are **El-Elyon – the Most High God**. You are supreme, the number one Ruler in the universe* **(b)** *and with You there is no partiality. (Ref.: Genesis 14:19-20; Psalm 83:18; Daniel 4:31-32; Colossians 3:23-25; 1 Peter 2:23; Romans 2:11.)*

Heart-to-heart
My will is good and perfect and I desire for you to know My will and to submit to My will that it may go well with you. Heaven and earth will pass away but My Words will not pass away; man's laws may change but Mine do not! I know what works and I know what does not work and choosing your will over My will does not work. You may think your way is working, but in essence it's stealing My best from you in this life and in the life to come. I am no respecter of persons but I am a respecter of obedience. Be not deceived, I have not come to take life from you; I have come to give life to you. (Ref.: Romans 12:1-2; Matthew 28:18-20; Deuteronomy 30:19-20. Matthew 24:35; John 1:1-4, 14; Hebrews 13:8; Malachi 3:6. Matthew 7:21-29. Proverbs 14:12; Matthew 16:24-26, 7:13-27; John 10:10-11; 1 Timothy 4:7-8; 1 Corinthians 15:16-20; 2 Corinthians 5:10. Acts 10:34; John 8:28-29; Romans 8:6-8; Romans 6:16-18; 1 John 3:22. John 8:31-36, 10:10-11.)

21(a) *You are **Yahweh-Tsidkenu – THE LORD MY RIGHTEOUSNESS**.* **(b)** *Jesus, I thank You that You were made to be sin Who knew no sin, that in and through You I might become [endued with, viewed as being in, and an example of] the righteousness of God [what I ought to be, approved and acceptable and in right relationship with You, by Your goodness]. (2 Corinthians 5:21-AMPCE.) (Ref.: Jeremiah 23:5-6.)*

Heart-to-heart
It's only through Christ and the life-giving flow of My Spirit that righteousness is born in the hearts of men. The wickedness that He took upon Himself was for you, My

child; My love for you is immeasurable and so too the price He paid for you to walk in righteousness and true holiness before Me. As you consider yourself dead to sin and alive to righteousness, keeping your eye single upon Me, you will be full of light and clearly see how to walk in newness of life. (Ref.: John 1:1-3, 14; Romans 5:13-21, 8:1-39; 1 John 2:29-3:9. 2 Corinthians 5:19-21; Isaiah 53:3-12; 1 Peter 2:21-25; Ephesians 3:14-21; Psalm 139:17-18; Romans 6:19; Ephesians 4:20-24. Romans 6:1-19; Philippians 3:8-14; Luke 11:33-36; Colossians 3:1-17; 2 Peter 1:19-21; Romans 6:4.)

22(a) *You are* **Yahweh-M'Kaddesh – You are the LORD who sanctifies**. **(b)** *You* sanctify [purify, consecrate, separate *me* for Yourself, *You* make *me* holy] by the Truth; Your Word is Truth. The sum of Your word is truth. (John 17:17-AMPCE; Psalm 119:160-AMPCE.) *(Ref.: Exodus 31:13; Leviticus 20:7-8; Hebrews 2:11, 9:11-18.)*

<u>Heart-to-heart</u>
My Words are spirit and they are life, the essence of who I Am. As you choose to renew your mind to My truths they will begin to expose ungodly thought patterns derived from your carnal nature. This is where true repentance takes place and cleansing from pollutants produced by sin. As you continue to renew your mind to My truths, My Word begins to form new patterns of thinking within you as it relates to the new man and My great love for you. I gave My life so that you can experience total sanctification—spirit, soul, and body: living out of My righteousness and holiness. (Ref.: John 6:63, 1:1-4, 14; John 8:58-NKJV. Romans 12:1-2 (renewing = Greek = renovation); 2 Corinthians 10:3-6; Hebrews 4:12-14. Matthew 15:10-20; John 17:17; Ephesians 5:25-27; Titus 3:3-7; Romans 7:14-8:8. Ephesians 4:20-24; Romans 8:29-39; 2 Corinthians 4:3-7, 3:15-18; Romans 12:1-2; John 8:31-36; Hebrews 13:20-21; Ephesians 3:17-19. John 3:16-17; 1 Thessalonians 5:23-24; Ephesians 4:20-24; Romans 6:22-23, 13:12-14.)

23(a) *You are* **Holy**. Holy is *Your* name, inspiring awe, reverence, and godly fear. **(b)** As the One Who called *me* is holy, *I choose to* be holy in all *my* conduct and manner of living, *by yielding to Your Word*. For it is written, "You shall be holy, for I am holy." **(c)** *I* cheerfully submit to, *You*, the Father of spirits, *so I may* [truly] live. For *You* discipline *me* for *my* certain good, that *I* may become a *partaker* of *Your* holiness. (Psalm 111:9-AMPCE; 1 Peter 1:15-16-AMPCE; Hebrews 12:9-10-AMPCE.) *(Ref.: 1 Peter 1:16; Ephesians 4:22-24.)*

♡ *Heart-to-heart*
I am Holy! There is nothing unclean or impure within Me! My thoughts, My Words, and My actions are clean and undefiled; therefore, My judgments and My ways are true and righteous. My Spirit has been given to you through the shed blood of My Son, Jesus, to bring you into a place of holiness: cleansing you from all filthiness of the flesh and spirit and creating within you a pure heart. Your choices in this life are essential in order to enter into My holiness. As you choose to submit your will to My ways, not in religious acts, but in fellowship with Me through prayer, worship, and renewing your mind to My truths, the sanctification process begins and continues; enjoying the reality of My presence and My promises through My Son. (Ref.: Leviticus 11:44-45; 1 Peter 1:15-16. Psalm 92:15; John 14:30. Psalm 92:15, 12:6; Hebrews 7:14-28; Revelation 16:7. John 7:37-39; Mark 7:15-23; 2 Corinthians 6:14-7:1; Ephesians 5:25-27; 1 Thessalonians 5:23; 2 Timothy 2:22. Romans 6:19-23; 1 Thessalonians 4:1-7. James 4:1-10; 1 Chronicles 16:11; Psalm 141:2; Romans 12:12; Ephesians 6:18; John 4:23-24; Romans 12:1-2; Ephesians 4:20-24; John 17:17, 19; Titus 3:3-7; Hebrews 8:1-13; 2 Corinthians 1:20-24.)

24(a) *You are* **Love.** **(b)** *Your love is given freely without any consideration of the merit or object of the person. Thank You that Your love for me is great! (Ref.: 1 John 4:8; John 3:16; Ephesians 2:1-10.)*

♡ *Heart-to-heart*
My love for you runs much deeper than your understanding can comprehend! You are valued because I love you; you cannot earn it as My Son paid the ultimate price for you to be able to receive it by My Spirit! Pride and selfishness cannot receive My love for My love is not self-seeking. Only a humble and submissive heart can receive Me and begin to enjoy My presence and My great love. My love resides in the depth of your being where your true essence is formed, identifying you as My child; no one on earth can love you in the perfect love that only I can give. (Ref.: Ephesians 3:14-21; John 3:16-21. Romans 8:15-39; John 7:37-39; Romans 5:1-8; John 7:37-39; 1 John 4:18-19. 1 Corinthians 13:1-13. 1 Peter 5:5-7; Isaiah 57:15; Ephesians 3:14-21; Colossians 2:6-7. Luke 11:9-13; John 4:1-14; Ephesians 3:14-21.)

25(a) *You prove Your love to me by being:* **Yahweh-Nissi – The LORD my banner.** **You are the standard of my victory in life's conflicts.** *Just as Moses lifted up the serpent in the desert [on a pole], so must the Son of Man be lifted up [on the cross], in order* that everyone who believes in *You* [who cleaves to *You*, trusts *You*, and relies on *You*] may not perish, but have eternal life and [actually] live forever! **(b)** *The cross of Christ is my banner of God's mighty power of redemption and is also the banner of my warfare, death to the old man—the false self.* (John 3:14-15-AMPCE.) (Ref.: Exodus 17:15; Isaiah 59:19; Numbers 21:1-9; Song of Solomon 2:4; Psalm 60:4-5, 111:7-9, 130:7-8; Galatians 6:14.)

♡ Heart-to-heart

Because of My obedience unto death, even the death of the cross, My name has been exalted above all else. Therefore, those who are in Me have nothing to fear for I have overcome the world. Redemption is yours through My shed blood; forgiveness is yours through My sacrifice; My wisdom and My prudence have been given to you in abundance. I am the firstborn, among many brethren, from the death of sin that was put upon Me as I hung on the cross. I am calling you to put to death the deeds of the flesh and to walk in newness of life. I have given to you exceedingly great and precious promises that you may be a partaker of My divine nature: for it is in Me that you live and move and have your being. I am faithful to My Words contained in the holy Scriptures; renew the spirit of your mind to My truths so you can enjoy all things that pertain to life and godliness. For if you walk in the Spirit you will not fulfill the lust of the flesh. (Ref.: Philippians 2:8-13. Acts 17:28; John 16:33. Romans 3:23-26; Ephesians 1:5-8; 1 Corinthians 1:30; Colossians 2:1-3; 2 Corinthians 4:6-7. Romans 8:29; 2 Corinthians 5:20-21. Romans 7:18-8:8; Romans 6:1-4. 2 Peter 1:1-11; Acts 17:28. 2 Timothy 3:16-17; Romans 12:1-2; Ephesians 4:20-24; 1 Peter 1:13; 2 Peter 1:1-11. John 6:63, 8:31-36; Galatians 5:16.)

26(a) *You are* the **Ancient of Days** [God, the eternal Father]. **(b)** *You are* the **Father of lights**. Every good gift and every perfect gift is from above; it comes down from *You*, the Father of all [that gives] light. **(c)** It is impossible for *You* ever to prove false or deceive *me*. (Daniel 7:9-AMPCE; James 1:17-AMPCE; Hebrews 6:18-AMPCE.) (Ref.: James 1:17.)

♡ Heart-to-heart

I am Alpha and Omega, the beginning and the end, the first and the last, the Almighty; in Me there is light and there is no darkness. As you surrender your heart and soul to Me confusion begins to dissipate; for he that follows after Me shall not walk in darkness but shall have the light of life. I gave My life as a ransom for you and yet so many do not fully understand the inheritance that is theirs through My sacrifice. For as Joshua led the children of Israel into the promised land as their inheritance, so My desire is for you to receive the inheritance of My kingdom. I laid down My life that you may walk in newness of life in Me. I am grieved that so many live in captivity because of deceitfulness of sin and stubbornness of heart. (Ref.: Revelation 22:13, 1:8; 1 John 1:1-10; Ecclesiastes 2:13-14. 1 Corinthians 14:33; John 8:12. Mark 10:45; John 10:14-18, 3:14-21; 2 Corinthians 3:18, 4:3-6. Joshua 1:1-11; Luke 17:21; John 18:35-36; 1 Corinthians 2:1-16. Romans 6:1-4; Acts 17:28. 1 Samuel 15:23; Hebrews 3:7-19.)

27(a) <u>*I* put away and rid *myself* [completely] of all these things: anger, rage, bad feeling toward others, curses and slander, and foulmouthed abuse and shameful utterances from *my* lips</u>, *and I do not lie to others.* <u>For *I* have stripped off the old (unregenerate) self *(the old man)* with its evil practices,</u> **(b)** and have clothed *myself* with the new [spiritual self] *(the new man)*, which is [ever in the process of being] renewed and remolded into [fuller and more perfect knowledge upon] knowledge after the image (the likeness) of Him Who created it. (Colossians 3:8-10-AMPCE.) *(Ref.: Ephesians 4:20-24.)*

♡ Heart-to-heart

Through My death, burial, and resurrection I have brought newness of life to you. For as the Holy Spirit and the power of the Most High came upon Mary to conceive Me, so too a miracle takes place inside of you—a new creation. As your spirit is born again and awakened, trust and faith in Me begins to grow as you feed on My Word, fellowship with Me through prayer and worship, and baring your heart to Me as a trusted friend; for I have called you to walk by faith and not by sight. I am the firstborn from the dead among many brethren which is the act of water baptism—dying to your carnal nature and living out of your new spiritual nature; for John indeed baptized with water, but I baptize you in My Spirit and fire. For as many of you as have been baptized into Christ have put on Christ. There is neither Jew nor Greek, bond nor free, male nor female; for you are all one in Me. And because you are Mine, you are Abraham's seed, and heirs according to the promise. (Ref.: Romans 6:1-18; 7:6. Luke 1:26-35; John 3:2-9; 1 Peter 1:22-23. 1 Peter 1:22-2:3; Hebrews 5:12-14; Luke 21:33-36; 1 Chronicles 16:11; Psalm 141;2, 142:1-2, 62:8; Philippians 4:6-7; 1 Peter 5:6-11; 2 Corinthians 5:6-7; Romans 1:16-17; 2 Corinthians 4:17-18. Romans 8:29; Acts 19:1-6; Ephesians 4:20-24; Romans 6:1-23; Luke 3:15-17. Galatians 3:27. Galatians 3:28. Galatians 3:29.)

🛑 If you have acted out of any carnal behavior patterns listed in 27(a) and you feel you need to journal your heart to your heavenly Father, please go to Chapter 5, Part Three. Being real with Him and releasing these to Him helps put off the old man. If you need to journal, you may not have

time right now. I want to encourage you when things arise, release them to Him. This is here to remind you of the importance of being real (honest) with the Lord. So, if you do not have anything to give to Him or do not have the time now, please continue...

28(a) *I* clothe *myself* therefore, as *one of* God's own chosen ones (*one of* His own picked representatives), [who are] purified and holy and well-beloved [by God Himself, by putting on behavior marked by] tenderhearted pity and mercy, kind feeling, humbleness of mind, gentle ways, [and] patience [which is tireless and long-suffering, and has the power to endure whatever comes, with good temper]. **(b)** *I am* gentle and forbearing with *others* and, if *I have* a difference (a grievance or complaint) against another, readily pardoning; even as *You, Lord, have* [freely] forgiven *me*, so must *I* also [forgive]. **(c)** Above all these things *I* put on *love*, which is the bond of perfectness. *And I* let the word of Christ dwell in *me* richly in all wisdom... (Colossians 3:12-13-AMPCE, 3:14, 16)*(Ref.: Colossians 3:12.)*

<u>Heart-to-heart</u>
Greater love has no man than this, that a man lay down his life for his friends. Selfishness and pride are not My ways for I am not self-seeking. My ways are higher than your ways; therefore, be wise and choose to clothe yourself with the righteousness that is born from above, allowing My light to penetrate your heart. (Ref.: John 15:13-14. 1 John 2:15-17; 1 Corinthians 13:1-13. Isaiah 55:7-11; James 3:13-18; Ephesians 4:20-24; Colossians 3:1-14; Hebrews 4:12-16; Psalm 119:130; 2 Peter 1:16-21.)

I want to encourage you to pray this to Him, "*Lord, let Your Words of truth penetrate my heart and my soul, dismantling the carnality within me, and bring forth the new man.*" Now, I want to encourage you to be quiet before the Lord for a few minutes communing with Him without spoken words.

Note:
- Where the word of a king is, there is power (Ecclesiastes 8:4; 1 Timothy 6:12-16).
- For the word of God is living and powerful, and sharper than any two-edged sword, piercing even to the division of soul and spirit, and of joints and marrow, and is a discerner of the thoughts and intents of the heart (Hebrews 4:12-NKJV).

Day Four

29(a) *Your* love has been poured out in *my heart* through *Your* Holy Spirit Who has been given to *me*. **(b)** *Your love is perfected in me and brought to completion because I treasure Your Word and love others.* **(c)** *I yield to Your love,* which springs from a pure heart and a good (clear) conscience and sincere (unfeigned) faith. (Romans 5:5-AMPCE; 1 Timothy 1:5-AMPCE.) *(Ref.: 1 John 2:5, 4:12.)*

Heart-to-heart
I am love, I am your treasure, and I desire to flow from your heart to others. I have come to remove the hardness from your heart and to cleanse you from sin and its damaging effects. I work within My people, My righteousness and My love one to the other. Do not be deceived, I have your best interest at heart and I know what's best for you. Trust Me with your life. (Ref.: 1 John 4:7-8; Ephesians 3:14-21; 2 Corinthians 4:5-7; Colossians 2:1-3; Ephesians 4:29-32; 1 Corinthians 13:1-13; Romans 13:10-14. Romans 2:28-29; Hebrews 12:14-17; 1 John 1:6-10; James 5:16-20; Hebrews 2:14-15; Matthew 15:11-20. Ephesians 4:20-24; Colossians 3:1-14; Ephesians 5:8-10; Galatians 5:22-26; Romans 13:8-10. Galatians 6:7-9; Romans 8:28-39; John 10:10; Hebrews 12:5-11; Jeremiah 29:11-14. 1 Peter 2:24-25.)

---

30. *So now, I put on love...*
- *Your* love *in me* endures long and is patient and kind.
- *Your* love *in me* rejoices in the truth.
- *Your* love *in me* bears all things. *It is a safe place for others.*
- *Your love in me* is ever ready to believe the best of every person. Its hopes are fadeless under all circumstances.
- *Your love in me* endures everything [without weakening].
- *Your* love *in me* never fails. (1 Corinthians 13:4-AMPCE, 13:6-7, 13:7-8-AMPCE.) *(Ref.: Colossians 3:14.)*

Heart-to-heart
It is My nature in you that is patient and kind, that rejoices when right and truth prevail, that covers and protects; My love in you endures all things. Strength and confidence are found in My perfect love and I desire that My very nature be the essence of your life. Allow Me to conform you into My image, to live in newness of life through regeneration and humbleness of mind. (Ref.: 1 Corinthians 13:4-8; 1 Peter 4:8; Ephesians 3:14-21; 2 Peter 1:1-11. 1 John 4:18; Luke 17:21; Romans 14:17; Nehemiah 8:10; Colossians 2:1-3; 2 Corinthians 4:6-7; Colossians 3:1-14; Ephesians 4:20-24;

Romans 12:1-2. Romans 8:29; 2 Corinthians 3:17-18; Romans 6:1-23; Colossians 3:1-14; Ephesians 4:20-24; Romans 12:1-2; Titus 3:4-7; 1 Peter 5:5-11.)

---

31. When I was a child, I talked like a child, I thought like a child, I reasoned like a child; now that I have become a *(wo)*man, I am done with childish ways and have put them aside, *so...*

- *Your* love *in me is not* envious nor boils over with jealousy.
- *Your love in me* is not boastful or vainglorious.
- *Your love in me* does not display itself haughtily.
- *Your love in me* is not conceited (*arrogant and inflated with pride*).
- *Your love in me* is not rude (unmannerly) and does not act unbecomingly.
- *Your* love *in me* does not insist on its own rights or its own way, for it is not self-seeking.
- *Your love in me* is not easily provoked [*it is not* overly sensitive *nor* easily angered].
- *Your love in me* thinks no evil. It takes no account of the evil done to it [it pays no attention to a suffered wrong].
- *Your love in me* does not rejoice in iniquity (*injustice and unrighteousness*), but rejoices in the truth. (1 Corinthians 13:11, 4, 5-AMPCE, 13:5-AMP, 13:5-6.)

♡ <u>*Heart-to-heart*</u>
I am calling you to put off your carnal behavior and be renewed in the spirit of your mind and to put on the new man, created after God in righteousness and true holiness. My body was broken and My blood was shed in order for you to be a partaker of My divine nature. I have come to give you life and that more abundantly. (Ref.: 1 Corinthians 3:1-3; Ephesians 4:20-24. 1 Corinthians 11:24-25; Matthew 26:26-28; John 3:14-20; 2 Peter 1:1-11; Romans 13:12-14; Galatians 3:26-29. John 10:10.)

32(a) Faith, hope, love abide, these three; but the greatest of these is love. *I* eagerly pursue and seek to acquire [this] love – *I* [make it *my* aim, *my* great quest]. **(b)** Love does no wrong to one's neighbor [it never hurts anybody]. <u>Therefore love meets all the requirements and is the fulfilling of the Law.</u> (1 Corinthians 13:13-14:1-AMPCE; Romans 13:10-AMPCE.)

♡ <u>*Heart-to-heart*</u>
Eagerly pursue and follow after My love—make it your aim, your great quest; for

there is nothing in heaven or on earth that is as precious or as powerful! You will grow strong in your inner man as you become rooted and built up in Me. I have said, "If you have faith as a grain of mustard seed, you shall say to this mountain, 'Move from here to there,' and it shall move; and nothing shall be impossible for you." The key for this kind of faith to work effectively is for you to be rooted and grounded in My love. The reality of My love in you brings to you worth, value, and confidence in Me. (Ref.: John 15:9-13; 1 Corinthians 13:1-8, 14:1-AMPCE; 1 Timothy 6:11-12. Ephesians 4:20-24; Colossians 2:6-7. Matthew 17:20; Mark 4:30-32. Galatians 5:6; Ephesians 3:14-21; 1 Corinthians 13:2. 1 John 4:18; Ephesians 3:1-21.)

33(a) *I* never return evil for evil or insult for insult (scolding, tongue-lashing, berating), but on the contrary blessing [praying for their welfare, happiness, and protection, and truly pitying and loving them]. For know that to this *I* have been called, that *I* may *myself* inherit a blessing [from God–that *I* may obtain a blessing as *an heir*, bringing welfare and happiness and protection]. **(b)** *For I want to* enjoy life and see good days [good–whether apparent or not], *so, I* keep *my* tongue free from evil and *my* lips from guile (treachery, deceit). James 3:2 reads, "…If any man offends not in word, the same is a perfect man *(fully developed in character)*…" **(c)** *I choose to be* quick to hear [a careful, thoughtful listener], slow to speak [a speaker of carefully chosen words and], slow to anger [patient, reflective, forgiving]; for the [resentful, deep-seated] anger of man does not produce the righteousness of God… (1 Peter 3:9-10-AMPCE; James 1:19-20-AMP.)

Heart-to-heart
You are created in My image and in My likeness. As I surrendered My will to the will of My Father in heaven, I am calling you to do the same in thought, purpose, and action. I came to give you life and that more abundantly; I did not come to condemn the world but that the world through Me might be saved. I am the Light of the world and I have called you to reveal My light to those around you through your words and your actions. Do not be conformed to this world, but be transformed by the renewing of your mind, that you may prove what is that good, perfect, and acceptable will of God. Trust yourself to your heavenly Father's care. (Ref.: Genesis 1:26-27; Romans 8:28-29; 1 Corinthians 15:45-49. Matthew 26:36-45; John 12:49-50; Colossians 3:1-17; Philippians 2:5-16. John 10:10, 3:16-17. John 1:6-18, 8:12; 1 Peter 2:9; Matthew 5:14-16; Ephesians 5:8-10; Galatians 5:22-26; 1 John 2:8-11. Romans 12:1-2; Luke 6:43-49; Habakkuk 2:4; Romans 1:17; Galatians 3:11; 2 Corinthians 4:17-18. 1 Peter 2:21-25; 1 Peter 5:5-7.)

34(a) *I let* nothing be done through strife or vainglory *(self-conceit)*; but in lowliness of mind *I* esteem others better than *myself*. *I* look out not only for *my* own interests, but also for the interests of others. *I am genuinely interested in the welfare of others. I seek to advance the interest of Jesus Christ and not my own.* **(b)** *I* do all things without murmurings and disputings: that *I* may be blameless and harmless, *a child* of God, without rebuke, in the midst of a crooked and perverse nation, among whom *I* shine as *a light* in the world; holding forth the word of life. (Philippians 2:3, 2:4-NKJV, 2:14-16.) (Ref.: Philippians 2:20-21.)

♡ Heart-to-heart
Renewing your mind is essential if you are to walk in My image and in My likeness! As you continue to feed on My Words of truth, ungodly thought patterns and mindsets that are rooted in the old man, your carnal nature, will be exposed. As you continue to allow My Words of truth to have preeminence in your life, they will take root within your heart and mind bringing forth the reality of the new man, My divine nature. It is My will for every member of My body to put on Christ. (Ref.: Romans 12:1-2; Ephesians 4:20-24; Colossians 3:10-11; 2 Corinthians 3:18; James 1:21-25. Mark 4:14-20; Luke 6:43-49; Hebrews 4:12-16. Ephesians 3:14-21; Colossians 2:6-15; Ephesians 4:20-24; 2 Peter 1:1-11. Romans 13:10-14; Galatians 3:26-29.)

---

35. *I* let this same attitude and purpose and [humble] mind be in *me* which was in Christ Jesus: *I* [let *You* be *my* example in humility]. (Philippians 2:5-AMPCE.)

♡ Heart-to-heart
As you surrender yourself to Me through prayer and renewing your mind to My truths, the renovation and transformation process begins. For in knowing Me you become like Me and there is nothing greater in this life. This is the only wise choice that is eternal. What is important in this life is who you are according to My righteousness and your obedience to My will. (Ref.: John 16:12-13, 6:63; Romans 8:5-29; 1 Peter 1:22-2:5; Romans 12:1-2. John 17:1-3; 1 Corinthians 15:45-49; Romans 12:1-2; 2 Corinthians 3:17-18; Romans 8:28-39. 1 Timothy 4:7-8; Matthew 7:13-14. 1 Timothy 4:7-8; 1 Corinthians 15:16-20; Isaiah 64:6-8; Ephesians 4:20-24; 2 Corinthians 5:10-21.)

36(a) [For my determined purpose is] that I may know *You* [that I may progressively become more deeply and intimately acquainted with *You*, perceiving and recognizing and understanding the wonders of *Your* Person more strongly and more clearly], and that I may in that same way come to know the power outflowing from *Your* resurrection [which it exerts over believers], **(b)** and that I may so share *Your* sufferings as to be continually transformed [in spirit into *Your* likeness even] to *Your* death, [in the hope] that if possible I may attain to the [spiritual and moral] resurrection [that lifts me] out from among the dead [even while in my body]. (Philippians 3:10-11-AMPCE.)

Heart-to-heart

As you choose to make knowing Me your determined purpose, things begin to change in your own personhood, as your identity becomes one with Me. I am no longer a religious activity in your life, but a life-giving force removing from you the strongholds that keep you bound to carnality and sin. The true treasure of My glory and eternal life is revealed to those who seek after Me with their whole heart. (Ref.: Philippians 3:3-11; 2 Corinthians 3:17-18; John 17:17-23. Romans 7:14-8:39; 1 Corinthians 3:1-7; 2 Corinthians 10:3-6; Hebrews 4:12-14. John 1:1-5, 14; 2 Corinthians 4:6-7, 3:17-18; Colossians 2:1-3; John 17:3; Hebrews 11:24-27; Jeremiah 29:11-13; Mark 12:28-34; Luke 10:25-28; Hebrews 11:6.)

37(a) *For* I have been crucified with Christ; it is no longer I who live, but Christ lives in me; **(b)** and the life which I now live in the flesh I live by faith in the Son of God, who loved me and gave Himself for me. (Galatians 2:20-NKJV.)

Heart-to-heart

I have called you to live by faith! Just as it takes time to build a house, so it takes time to build a life of faith. As you commit to seek after Me and put Me first place in your life, My Spirit of truth works in you to reveal and to remove ungodliness and darkness. The light of My Word permeates your very being and you begin to grow in faith. Through this process, your carnal nature loses its strength and authority in your life: becoming a vessel of honor, a temple of light to shine through you to others, bringing glory to Me. (Ref.: Romans 1:17; 2 Corinthians 5:5-7; Galatians 2:20-21, 6:14. Mark 4:26-33; Luke 6:46-49. Matthew 6:19-34; John 6:63, 16:13; Hebrews 4:12-16; 2 Corinthians 10:3-6; Colossians 1:9-18; Ephesians 2. Psalm 119:130; 2 Peter 1:17-21; 1 Peter 2:1-3; Romans 10:17; 2 Peter 3:17-18. Romans 8:5-6; 1 Corinthians 15:55-58; 2 Timothy 2:19-21; 1 Corinthians 6:19-20; 2 Corinthians 4:6-18; Ephesians 5:8-10; Matthew 5:13-16.)

🛑 I want to encourage you to pray this to Him, *"Lord, let Your Words of truth penetrate my heart and my soul, dismantling the carnality within me, and bring forth the new man."* Now, I want to encourage you to be quiet before the Lord for a few minutes communing with Him without spoken words.

Note:
- Where the word of a king is, there is power (Ecclesiastes 8:4; 1 Timothy 6:12-16).
- For the word of God is living and powerful, and sharper than any two-edged sword, piercing even to the division of soul and spirit, and of joints and marrow, and is a discerner of the thoughts and intents of the heart (Hebrews 4:12-NKJV).

SCRIPTURES DESIGNED TO HELP PUT ON THE NEW MAN CONCERNING:

B. Work Ethics, Submission to Authority, and Entering into His Sufferings

Along with corresponding words of wisdom from the Lord

-Heart-to-heart-

"But Jesus called them to him, and sayeth unto them, 'Ye know that they which are accounted to rule over the Gentiles exercise lordship over them; and their great ones exercise authority upon them. But so shall it not be among you: but whosoever will be great among you, shall be your minister: and whosoever of you will be the chiefest, shall be servant of all. For even the Son of man came not to be ministered unto, but to minister, and to give his life a ransom for many.'" Mark 10:42-45

"Servants, be obedient to them that are your masters according to the flesh, with fear and trembling, in singleness of your heart, as unto Christ; not with eyeservice, as menpleasers; but as the <u>servants of Christ</u>, doing the will of God from the heart; with good will doing service, as to the Lord, and not to men: knowing that whatsoever good thing any man doeth, the same shall he receive of the Lord, whether he be bond or free." Ephesians 6:5-8

"And whatsoever ye do in word or deed, do all in the name of the Lord Jesus, giving thanks to God and the Father by him." Colossians 3:17

"Servants, obey in all things your masters according to the flesh; not with eyeservice, as menpleasers; but in singleness of heart, fearing God: and whatsoever ye do, do it heartily, as to the Lord, and not unto men; knowing that of the Lord ye shall receive the reward of the inheritance: for ye serve the Lord Christ. But he that doeth wrong shall receive for the wrong which he hath done: and there is no respect of persons." Colossians 3:22-25

"Exhort servants to be obedient to their own masters, and to please them well in all things; not answering again; not purloining, but shewing all good fidelity; that they may adorn the doctrine of God our Saviour in all things." Titus 2:9-10

Day Five

38(a) Whatever *I* do [no matter what it is] in word or deed, *I* do everything in the name of the Lord Jesus and in [dependence upon] His Person, giving praise to God the Father through Him. *I obey those who are in authority over me*, not only when their eyes are on *me* as pleasers of men, but in simplicity of purpose [with all my heart] because of my reverence for *You, Lord,* and as a sincere expression of *my* devotion to *You. So,* whatever may be *my* task, I work at it heartily (from the soul), as [something done] for the Lord and not for men, knowing [with all certainty] that it is from the Lord [and not from men] that *I* will receive the inheritance which is *my* [real] reward. [The One Whom] *I'm* actually serving [is] the Lord Christ (the Messiah). For he who deals wrongfully will [reap the fruit of his folly and] be punished for his wrongdoing. **(b)** And [with God] there is no partiality [no matter what a person's position may be… (Colossians 3:17, 22-25-AMPCE.) *(Ref.: Titus 3:1-2.)*

♡♡ *Heart-to-heart*
You have been bought with a price, therefore glorify Me in your body and in your spirit, which are Mine. As Jesus, who is the Light of the world, came to serve, so too I am calling you to be a light in all that you do in word and in deed. Just as David was a man after My own heart and the outward manifestation of his love and honor for Me was seen in his faithfulness in the tasks set before him; I am calling you to be faithful in the tasks that are before you. As I was with David and exalted him, I reward those whose hearts are toward Me. (Ref.: 1 Corinthians 6:19-20, 7:22-24. John 1:6-18, 8:12; Mark 10:42-45; Matthew 5:13-16; Colossians 3:17, 23-24; 1 Corinthians 10:31; Ephesians 5:8-10. Acts 13:20-23; 1 Samuel 13:13-14, 17:15-22, 34-37, 18:14, 30; Matthew 25:14-46; Colossians 3:23-24. Hebrews 11:6.)

---

39. *I am submissive to those who are in authority over me* with all [proper] respect, not only to those who are kind and considerate and reasonable, but also to those who are surly (overbearing, unjust, and crooked). For one is regarded favorably if, as in the sight of God, he endures the pain of unjust suffering. [After all] what kind of glory [is there in it] if, when *I* do wrong and are punished for it, *I* take it patiently? But if *I* bear patiently with suffering [which results] when *I* do right and that is undeserved, it is acceptable and pleasing to God. For even to this *I have been* called [it is inseparable from my vocation]. For Christ also suffered for me, leaving me [His personal] example, so that *I* should follow in His footsteps. He was guilty of no sin, neither was deceit (guile) ever found on His lips. When He was reviled and insulted, He did not revile or offer insult in return; [when] He was abused and suffered, He made no threats [of vengeance]; but He trusted [Himself and everything] to *His heavenly Father* Who judges *righteously*. (1 Peter 2:18-23-AMPCE.) *(Ref.: Titus 2:9-3:2; 1 Peter 2:23.)*

40. *Father, today, I trust myself and everything to You who judges righteously. (Ref.: 1 Peter 2:23)*

♡ *Heart-to-heart*
I have called you to live out of a place greater than your physical senses; I have called you to live out of your born-again spirit man. In this new creation I dwell: My peace, My wisdom, My strength, My protection. As you learn to dwell and remain in this place, while your soul may suffer in this life, you remain with Me in a place of peace. I have called you to be a light in a dark world. As Jesus walked in humbleness of mind, I am calling you to do the same. Fear not for I am your confidence, I am your peace, I am your strong tower of refuge; pour out your heart to Me, for I care for you and I am a very present help in times of trouble. (Ref.: 2 Corinthians 4:6-18; Ephesians 4:20-24; Colossians 3:1-14; 2 Corinthians 3:17-18; James 1:21-25. Luke 17:20-21; Romans 14:17; Colossians 1:27; John 14:23-28, 16:33; 2 Corinthians 4:6-7; Colossians 2:1-3; 1 Corinthians 1:23-24; 1 Peter 2:24-25. 2 Corinthians 4:8-18; 1 Peter 4:15-19, 5:10; John 14:23-28, 16:33; Romans 8:6; Philippians 4:6-9. Matthew 5:14-16; 1 John 2:10-11. Philippians 2:5-13; 1 Peter 5:5-11. Philippians 3:3; John 14:21-27, 16:33; Proverbs 18:10; Psalm 62:7-8, 142:1-2; 1 Peter 5:6-10; Psalm 46:1-5; 1 Peter 2:24-25.)

---

41. [*I see to it that*] *my* conscience is entirely clear (unimpaired), so that, when *I am* falsely accused as *an evildoer*, those who threaten *me* abusively and revile *my* right behavior in Christ may come to be ashamed [of slandering *my* good *life*]. For [it is] better to suffer [unjustly] for doing right, if that should be God's will, than to suffer [justly] for doing wrong. For Christ [the Messiah Himself] died for sins once for all, the Righteous for the unrighteous (the Just for the unjust, the Innocent for the guilty), that He might bring us to God. In His human body He was put to death, but He was made alive *by the Spirit*. (1 Peter 3:16-18-AMPCE.) *(Ref.: 1 Peter 3:18.)*

♡ *Heart-to-heart*
The mystery of faith is held in a pure conscience. My Words are alive and powerful, and as you feed on My Word and act on My Word a cleansing takes place within your mind and your conscience. Faith begins to work deep within your soul and your trust in Me becomes evident to others. It pleases Me when I see your faith in operation in difficult

situations as I see the image of My Son in you. I am faithful to My Word—I will never leave you nor forsake you. (Ref.: 1 Timothy 3:9. Hebrews 4:12-14; Titus 1:15; James 1:21-25; 1 John 1:5-9; 2 Corinthians 7:1; Acts 24:16. Matthew 7:24-27, 16:13-18, 5:14-16. Romans 8:14-18; 1 Peter 2:18-25; 2 Corinthians 4:17-18; 1 Peter 5:6-11; 2 Corinthians 3:17-18; 1 Peter 4:14-19. 2 Corinthians 1:20; Hebrews 13:5-6.)

---

42. So, since Christ suffered in the flesh for *me*, *I* arm *myself* with the same thought and purpose [patiently to suffer rather than fail to please God]. For whoever has suffered in the flesh [having the mind of Christ] is done with [intentional] sin [has stopped pleasing himself and the world, and pleases God], so *I* can no longer spend the rest of my natural life living by [*my*] human appetites and desires, but [*I live*] for what God wills. (1 Peter 4:1-2-AMPCE.)

Heart-to-heart
I am calling you to a higher life that can only be found in Me. The carnal mind cannot understand it because it goes against the very fabric of what seems to be right. Loving your enemies, doing good to those who hate you, blessing those who curse you, and praying for those who despitefully use you does not seem right to the carnal way of thinking. There is suffering that takes place in those who choose to take up their cross and follow Me and My glory is revealed to those in this life and in the life to come. (Ref.: 1 John 5:11; John 17:3; Colossians 3:1-4; Ephesians 2:1-10. Proverbs 14:12; Romans 8:1-8. Matthew 5:44-48, 18:21-35; Romans 12:1-2; John 18:36; 1 John 2:15-17. Mark 8:34-38; Galatians 2:20-21; Romans 8:16-19; Matthew 7:13-14; 1 Corinthians 2:6-12; 2 Corinthians 3:7-18; 1 Timothy 4:7-8; 1 Corinthians 15:16-20; 2 Corinthians 5:10.)

---

43. *I* also choose to let *my character* be without covetousness; and *I am* content with such things as *I* have: for *You have* said, "I will never leave *you*, nor forsake *you*." So that *I* may boldly say, "The Lord is my helper, and I will not fear what man shall do unto me." (Hebrews 13:5-6.)

Heart-to-heart
Do not be deceived! Discern clearly and beware of covetousness for a man's life consists not in the abundance of the things which he possesses. True riches and abundant life are found only in Me. Do not get caught up with seeking after what the nations of this world seek after, for your heavenly Father knows that you have need. Be wise and seek the kingdom of God and His righteousness and all these things will be added unto

you; for it is your Father's good pleasure to give you the kingdom. But know this, the man whose focus is on the cares of this world, deceitfulness of riches, and lust for other things causes My Word to be of no effect in his life; it will not produce fruit. Trust Me to meet your needs! Stay focused on Me and cast all your care upon Me, for I care for you. (Ref.: Galatians 6:7. Luke 12:13-21, 16:10-11; Ephesians 3:8-19; John 10:10; Acts 17:28. Luke 12:22-30. Luke 12:31-32; Ephesians 5:14-17. Mark 4:1-19; Galatians 5:22-24. Psalm 23; Philippians 4:19; Hebrews 13:5-6. Hebrews 12:1-2; 1 Peter 5:6-11, 2:24-25.)

🛑 Where applicable, please continue with C and D. Otherwise, I want to encourage you to pray this to Him, "*Lord, let Your Words of truth penetrate my heart and my soul, dismantling the carnality within me, and bring forth the new man.*" Now, I want to encourage you to be quiet before the Lord for a few minutes communing with Him without spoken words.

Note:
- Where the word of a king is, there is power (Ecclesiastes 8:4; 1 Timothy 6:12-16).
- For the word of God is living and powerful, and sharper than any two-edged sword, piercing even to the division of soul and spirit, and of joints and marrow, and is a discerner of the thoughts and intents of the heart (Hebrews 4:12-NKJV).

SCRIPTURES DESIGNED TO HELP PUT ON THE NEW MAN CONCERNING:

C. Marriage

Along with corresponding words of wisdom from the Lord

Heart-to-heart

"Wives, submit yourselves unto your own husbands, as unto the Lord. For the husband is the head of the wife, even as Christ is the head of the church: and he is the saviour of the body. Therefore as the church is subject unto Christ, so let the wives be to their own husbands in every thing." Ephesians 5:22-24

"Husbands, love your wives, even as Christ also loved the church, and gave himself for it; that he might sanctify and cleanse it with the washing of water by the word, that he might present it to himself a glorious church, not having spot, or wrinkle, or any such thing; but that it should be holy and without blemish. So ought men to love their wives as their own bodies. He that loveth his wife loveth himself. For no man ever yet hated his own flesh; but nourisheth and cherisheth it, even as the Lord the church: for we are members of his body, of his flesh, and of his bones." Ephesians 5:25-30

"Wives, submit yourselves unto your own husbands, as it is fit in the Lord." Colossians 3:18

"Husbands, love your wives, and be not bitter against them." Colossians 3:19

"Likewise, ye wives, be in subjection to your own husbands; that, if any obey not the word, they also may without the word be won by the conversation (behavior) of the wives; while they behold your chaste conversation (behavior) coupled with fear. Whose adorning let it not be that outward adorning of plaiting the hair, and of wearing of gold, or of putting on of apparel; but let it be the hidden man of the heart, in that which is not corruptible, even the ornament of a meek and quiet spirit, which is in the sight of God of great price. For after this manner in the old time the holy women also, who trusted in God, adorned themselves, being in subjection unto their own husbands: even as Sara obeyed Abraham, calling him lord: whose daughters ye are, as long as ye do well, and are not afraid with any amazement (fear or alarm)." 1 Peter 3:1-6

"Likewise, ye husbands, dwell with them according to knowledge, giving honour unto the wife, as unto the weaker vessel, and as being heirs together of the grace of life; that your prayers be not hindered." 1 Peter 3:7

My Responsibility as a Wife
(Fill in blanks with husband's name)

Day Five (If applicable, please continue)
44(a) Ephesians 5:22-24 (AMPCE) reads, "Wives, be subject (be submissive and adapt yourselves) to your own husbands as [a service] to the Lord. For the husband is head of the wife as Christ is the Head of the church, Himself the Savior of [His] body. As the church is subject to Christ, so let wives also be subject in everything to their husbands." *So, as* _____ *wife, I am* subject to *him*, [*I* subordinate and adapt *myself* to *him*], as is right and fitting and *my* proper duty in the Lord, so that even if *he does* not obey the Word [of God], *he* may be won over not by discussion but by the [godly] *life in which he sees in me*. When *he* observes the pure and modest way in which *I* conduct *myself*, together with *my* reverence [for *him*…]. *I* let *it* not be the [merely] external adorning with [elaborate] interweaving and knotting of the hair, the wearing of jewelry, or changes of clothes; but *I let it be* the hidden man of the heart *(the new man)*, in that which is not corruptible, *even the ornament* of a meek and quiet spirit, which is in the sight of God of great price. **(b)** For in this manner, in former times, the holy women who trusted in God also adorned themselves, being submissive to their own husbands. It was thus that Sarah obeyed Abraham [following his guidance and acknowledging his headship over her by] calling him lord. And *I am* her true daughter *because I* do right and let nothing terrify *me* [*I do* not *give* way to hysterical fears or let anxieties unnerve *me*]. *My trust is in You, Lord!* (Colossians 3:18-AMPCE; 1 Peter 3:1-3-AMPCE, 3:4, 3:5-NKJV, 3:6-AMPCE.) *(Ref.: 1 Peter 2:21-23.)*

Heart-to-heart
Daughter, I love you and you are very valuable to Me! I have called you to be a reflection of My character and nature to your husband, your family, and to all you come in contact with. A good gift—the hidden man of the heart, a meek and quiet spirit whose total trust is in Me! Your submission and strength is found as you look to Me in your calling as a wife. It pleases Me when you choose to inwardly adorn yourself with the truth of My Word as it brings forth light to your spirit man and to those around you. Even in the midst of chaos and darkness, My light within you brings righteousness, peace, and joy. Be of good cheer for I have overcome the world. (Ref.: Ephesians 3:14-21; Psalm 139:13-18; John 3:16-17. Acts 17:28; Romans 8:35-39; Galatians 3:27-29; Ephesians 5:8-10; Galatians 5:22-25. Ephesians 4:20-24. 1 Peter 2:18-3:4; Isaiah 32:17; Proverbs 31:10-31; Psalm 18:2, 32. 1 Peter 3:3-5; Titus 2:10; Colossians 3:10; Ephesians 4:20-24; Psalm 119:130; Proverbs 20:27; Luke 11:34; Proverbs 31:18; Matthew 5:14-16. Titus

2:9-14; Ephesians 6:10-18; 1 Thessalonians 5:3-10; 2 Samuel 22:29-37; Psalm 18:28, 119:130; Romans 14:17. John 16:33.)

---

45. Proverbs 21:9 (AMPCE) and 19 reads, "It is better to dwell in a corner of the housetop [on the flat oriental roof, exposed to all kinds of weather] than in a house shared with a <u>nagging, quarrelsome, and faultfinding woman</u>. *It is* better to dwell in the wilderness, than with a contentious and an angry woman." *(Continue to) help me see my faults and to examine my own heart so that I may be an example of Your character and nature to my family. I desire to be an example of the true bride of Christ, by allowing You to sanctify and wash me with the water of Your Word. Let Your Word that I am speaking, which is alive and full of power, go into the deepest parts of my nature to expose, sift, analyze, and judge the very thoughts and purposes of my heart. (Ref.: 2 Corinthians 13:5; Ephesians 5:25-26; Hebrews 4:12.)*

♡ Heart-to-heart

Daughter, My will for you is to walk and live in righteousness, peace, and joy, not in fear, pain, and bitterness. My death on the cross has made it possible for Me, by My Word and through the power of My Spirit, to go into the depths of your soul to free you from all the works of the devil who wants to keep you from the very life that I died to give to you. Stop believing his lies and surrender to Me; release your pain and insecurities to Me and all who have affected you in negative ways and I will help you find the freedom and joy that your heart longs for. Forgive others and yourself; confess your faults before Me and mature others in My body, and healing will begin to take place within your own soul. I am the fountain of living waters and I have come to give you life and that more abundantly. (Ref.: Romans 14:17; 2 Timothy 1:7; Hebrews 12:14-15; 2 Corinthians 10:3-6. Hebrews 4:12-14; John 7:37-39; Luke 6:45-49; Colossians 2:12-15; 1 John 3:8, 4:18; John10:10. John 8:44; 2 Corinthians 10:3-6; Colossians 1:9-17; Romans 8:5-19, 31-39; Ephesians 4:20-32; Romans 12:1-2; Psalm 62:8, 142:1-2; 1 Peter 5:6-11; John 8:31-36; 1 Peter 2:24-25; 2 Corinthians 5:21; Romans 14:17; Luke 12:22-32. Matthew 6:9-15; Mark 11:25-26; Luke 6:35-37; 1 John 1:7-10; Galatians 5:22-24; James 5:16-20. Jeremiah 2:13; John 4:13-14, 7:38-39; Revelation 21:6; John 10:10.)

🛑 If you have been nagging, quarrelsome, and/or faultfinding toward your husband or have acted out of any carnal behavior patterns listed in 27(a) and you feel you need to journal your heart to your heavenly Father, please go to Chapter 5, Part Three. Being real (honest) with Him and releasing these acts to Him helps put off the old man. If you need to journal, you

may not have the time right now. I want to encourage you when things arise, release them to Him. This is here to remind you of the importance of being real (honest) with the Lord. So, if you do not have anything to give to Him, or if you do not have the time now, please continue...

Note: A prayer of repentance is included in Chapter 6.

---

46. *I thank You that* _____ *loves me, as You, Lord,* loved the church and gave *Yourself* up for her, so that *You* might sanctify her, having cleansed her by the washing of water with the Word, that *You* might present the church to *Yourself* in glorious splendor, without spot or wrinkle or any such things [that she might be holy and faultless]. Even so, *my husband loves me* as [being in a sense] *his* own *body.* He who loves his own wife loves himself. For no man ever hated his own flesh, but nourishes and carefully protects and cherishes it, as Christ does the church. _____ *is* [affectionate and sympathetic with *me*]; *he is not* harsh or bitter or resentful toward *me. He lives* considerately with [*me*], with an intelligent recognition [of the marriage relation], honoring *me* as [physically] the weaker, but [realizing that *we*] are joint heirs of the grace (God's unmerited favor) of life, in order that *our* prayers may not be hindered and cut off. [Otherwise we cannot pray effectively]. (Ephesians 5:25-29-AMPCE; Colossians 3:19-AMPCE; 1 Peter 3:7-AMPCE.)

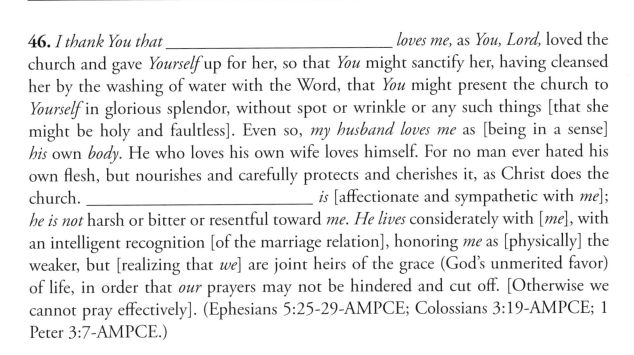 **If applicable, please continue with D. Otherwise, I want to encourage you to pray this to Him,** *"Lord, let Your words of truth penetrate my heart and my soul, dismantling the carnality within me, and bring forth the new man."* **Now, I want to encourage you to be still before the Lord for a few minutes communing with Him without spoken words.**

Note:
- *Where the word of a king is, there is power (Ecclesiastes 8:4; 1 Timothy 6:12-16).*
- *For the word of God is living and powerful, and sharper than any two-edged sword, piercing even to the division of soul and spirit, and of joints and marrow, and is a discerner of the thoughts and intents of the heart (Hebrews 4:12-NKJV).*

My Responsibility as a Husband
(Fill in blanks with wife's name)

Day Five (If applicable, please continue)

47. As _____ *husband, I love her as You, Lord,* loved the church and gave *Yourself* up for her, so that *You* might sanctify her, having cleansed her by the washing of water with the Word, that *You* might present the church to *Yourself* in glorious splendor, without spot or wrinkle or any such things [that she might be holy and faultless]. Even so *I* love _____ as [being in a sense] *my* own *body. For* he who loves his own wife loves himself. For no man ever hated his own flesh, but nourishes and carefully protects and cherishes it, as Christ does the church. *I am* [affectionate and sympathetic with *her*] and *I am* not harsh or bitter or resentful toward *her. I* live considerately with _____, with an intelligent recognition [of the marriage relation], honoring *her* as [physically] the weaker, but [realizing that *we*] are joint heirs of the grace (God's unmerited favor) of life, in order that *our* prayers may not be hindered and cut off. [Otherwise we cannot pray effectively]. (Ephesians 5:25-29-AMPCE; Colossians 3:19-AMPCE; 1 Peter 3:7-AMPCE.)

Heart-to-heart

Son, I love you and only I can fill the deep longings of your heart! I gave Myself for you to sanctify and cleanse you in order for your life to be a reflection of My character and nature to your wife, your family, and to all you come in contact with. Do not allow pride and selfishness to keep you from the abundant life that can only be found in Me. I want to free you from your fears, pain, heartache, loneliness, resentment, bitterness, and unforgiveness. I have called you to be a good gift to your wife, to love her as I love you; revealing to her My love, My mercy, My forgiveness, My faithfulness, and My patience. Let her see Me and the vastness of My love through you—My love never fails! As you love your wife, you love yourself and honor Me. (Ref.: Galatians 4:4-7; Ephesians 3:14-21; Romans 8:35-39; 2 Peter 1:1-11; John 7:37-39. 1 John 1:6-10; 1 Thessalonians 5:23-24; Hebrews 13:12; James 1:22-25; Ephesians 5:8-10, 25-33; Galatians 5:22-25; 2 Corinthians 3:17-18. Proverbs 28:25; James 4:6-8; 1 Peter 5:5-11; Mark 4:13-20; John 10:10. 1 John 3:8, 4:18; Hebrews 2:14-18, 12:14-16; Luke 4:18-19; Matthew 6:9-15. James 1:16-20; Colossians 3:1-17, 19; Romans 12:1-2; Galatians 5:16-25. 1 Corinthians 13:1-8, 14:1; 2 Corinthians 3:17-18; James 1:21-25; Psalm 128:1-4; Ephesians 3:14-19; Romans 8:32-39. Ephesians 5:28-30.)

🛑 If you have been harsh, bitter, or resentful toward your wife or have acted out of any carnal behavior patterns listed in 27(a) and you feel you need to journal your heart to your heavenly Father, please go to Chapter 5, Part Three. Being real with Him and releasing these acts to Him helps put off the old man. If you need to journal, you may not have the time right now. I want to encourage you when things arise, release them to Him. This is here to remind you of the importance of being real (honest) with the Lord. So, if you do not have anything to give to Him or if you do not have the time now, please continue…

Note: A prayer of repentance is included in Chapter 6.

---

48. *I thank You that* _____ *is* subject to *me, she [subordinates* and *adapts herself to me], as is right and fitting and her proper duty in the Lord. As the church is subject to Christ, so* _____ *also is* subject *to me in everything.* (Colossians 3:18-AMPCE; Ephesians 5:24-AMPCE.)

🛑 If applicable, please continue with D. Otherwise, I want to encourage you to pray this to Him, *"Lord, let Your Words of truth penetrate my heart and my soul, dismantling the carnality within me, and bring forth the new man."* Now, I want to encourage you to be quiet before the Lord for a few minutes communing with Him without spoken words.

Note:
- Where the word of a king is, there is power (Ecclesiastes 8:4; 1 Timothy 6:12-16).
- For the word of God is living and powerful, and sharper than any two-edged sword, piercing even to the division of soul and spirit, and of joints and marrow, and is a discerner of the thoughts and intents of the heart (Hebrews 4:12-NKJV).

SCRIPTURES DESIGNED TO HELP PUT ON THE NEW MAN CONCERNING:

D. Family

Along with corresponding words of wisdom from the Lord

-Heart-to-heart-

"Children, obey your parents in the Lord: for this is right. Honour thy father and mother; (which is the first commandment with promise;) that it may be well with thee, and thou mayest live long on the earth." Ephesians 6:1-3

"And, ye fathers, provoke not your children to wrath: but bring them up in the nurture and admonition of the Lord." Ephesians 6:4

"Children, obey your parents in all things: for this is well pleasing unto the Lord." Colossians 3:20

"Fathers, provoke not your children to anger, lest they be discouraged." Colossians 3:21

My Responsibility as a Parent
(circle the applicable pronouns)

Day Five (If applicable, please continue)
49. *I thank You that* _____(mom or dad's name)_____ *and I do not irritate and provoke our child/children to anger we* [*do not exasperate him/her/them to resentment*]. *We are* [*not hard on him/her/them or harass him/her/them*], *lest he/she/they become(s) discouraged and sullen and morose and feel(s) inferior and frustrated. We* [*do not break his/her/their spirit*], *but we rear him/her/them* [*tenderly*] *in the training and discipline and the counsel and admonition of the Lord.* (Ephesians 6:4-AMPCE; Colossians 3:21-AMPCE; Ephesians 6:4-AMPCE.)

Heart-to-heart
Children are a blessing to Me. Their innocence and tenderness of heart represents the kingdom of God and I have called you to represent Me to them. I desire for children to know Me at a very young age, to understand My character and nature: that I am slow to anger and plenteous in mercy and loving-kindness. Draw life from Me so you can impart My life to your children. Let them see the fruit of living out of the new man, as a child's heart finds safety in that environment as they behold your strength of character. Release your disappointments and frustrations to Me and trust Me as your inner man grows stronger. I desire to reveal Myself to you and in turn to your children. (Ref.: Matthew 19:13-14. Matthew 18:1-6; Ephesians 6:4; Deuteronomy 6:4-7-AMPCE; Genesis 18:17-19. Psalm 103:8-13, 145:8-9; Proverbs 14:29, 15:18, 16:32. John 6:63, 7:37-39; Romans 8:5-6. Ephesians 4:20-24; Colossians 3:1-21; 2 Corinthians 3:17-18; Galatians 5:16-26; Ephesians 5:8-10; Philippians 3:9. Psalm 62:8, 142:1-2; 1 Peter 5:6-11, 2:1-5; 2 Peter 1:1-11. John 14:20-27, 17:17-23; 1 Corinthians 2:9-16; Philippians 2:5; Deuteronomy 6:4-7-AMPCE.)

If you have been hard on your child(ren) and you feel you need to journal your heart to your heavenly Father, please go to Chapter 5, Part Three. Being real with Him and releasing these acts to Him helps put off the old man. If you need to journal, you may not have the time right now. I want to encourage you when things arise, release them to Him. This is here to remind you of the importance of being real (honest) with the Lord. So, if you do not have anything to give to Him or if you do not have the time now, please continue…

Note: A prayer of repentance is included in Chapter 6.

My Child(ren)'s Responsibility
(circle the applicable pronouns)

50. *I thank You that _____(child(ren)'s name(s))_____ obey(s) ___(mom or dad's name)___ and me in the Lord [as His representatives], for this is just and right and it is pleasing to You. _____(child(ren)'s name(s))_____ honor(s) (esteem(s) and value(s) as precious) his/her/their father and his/her/their mother–this is the first commandment with a promise–that all may be well with him/her/them and that he/she/they may live long on the earth. (Ephesians 6:1-3-AMPCE.) (Ref.: Colossians 3:20)*

<3 *Heart-to-heart*
My child, I formed you in your mother's womb, you are unique and there is no one like you; I gave you your own fingerprints and your own personality. I love you and you are not alone; I am with you always—when you sleep, when you awake, when you are at school, when you are playing, when you are fearful, when you are hurting; I am with you. You are very special and valuable to Me, and when you share your heart with Me, I listen, for I care for you. I did not bring you forth to walk in rebellion or defiance, but in innocence and humbleness of mind and heart before Me. It is My will for you to honor your father and your mother from which you came, and to seek Me and to know Me; for in Me you will find life and peace. (Ref.: Psalm 139:1-18. John 3:16-17; Romans 8:31-39; Hebrews 13:5; Matthew 10:29-31. Matthew 18:1-6; Psalm 62:8; 1 Peter 5:6-7. Proverbs 15:5, 20, 17:21, 19:26, 20:20, 30:11-12; Matthew 19:13-14. Ephesians 6:1-3; John 17:3; Matthew 6:22-34; John 6:63, Romans 8:6; John 10:10.)

STOP **I want to encourage you to pray this to Him,** *"Lord, let Your Words of truth penetrate my heart and my soul, dismantling the carnality within me, and bring forth the new man."* **Now, I want to encourage you to be quiet before the Lord for a few minutes communing with Him without spoken words.**

Note:
- Where the word of a king is, there is power (Ecclesiastes 8:4; 1 Timothy 6:12-16).
- For the word of God is living and powerful, and sharper than any two-edged sword, piercing even to the division of soul and spirit, and of joints and marrow, and is a discerner of the thoughts and intents of the heart (Hebrews 4:12-NKJV).

Chapter 5
PERSONAL PRAYER JOURNAL
From your heart to His

Details and Instructions

Details:
Question: What do you do with worries, fears, and anxieties of the heart? Some people go to a psychiatrist to help cope with life or turn to drugs and/or alcohol to help numb the disappointments of life and the pain and wounding of the heart. Others live out of their carnal behavior patterns and mindsets by acting out of their feelings and emotions. I have found that the following two disciplines have been life-changing for me, bringing much victory in my life:

1. Being real with my Lord, my heavenly Father, and His Holy Spirit through journaling the specific situations and/or circumstances that have triggered ungodly behavior or thought patterns. For an example, please see Exhibit C (Isaiah 9:6).

2. Renewing the *spirit of my mind* or my *inmost mind* to the truth of God's Word concerning the new man in Christ. (See **My Story – Part Two**, Chapter 2, and the **Personalized Scripture Guide – Details and Directives**, Chapter 4).

Through these two disciplines, instead of a narcissistic stronghold of pride along with the deep feelings of insecurity and self-rejection, the Lord and His truth have become my stronghold and strength (Psalm 18:2; Proverbs 10:29; Nahum 1:7).

Hebrews 12:15 reads – *Looking diligently lest any man fail of the grace of God; lest any root of bitterness trouble you, and thereby many be defiled.* The phrase "looking diligently" in the Greek is *episkopeo* meaning "to oversee; by implication, to beware:– look diligently, take the oversight." It is our responsibility to take the oversight and to be aware of our own emotional and mental activities. God holds us accountable! We must do our due diligence to guard our minds, our emotions, and our hearts from ungodly influences. Proverbs 4:23 (NIV) reads – *"Above all else, guard your heart, for everything you do flows from it."* The Greek word for "heart" is *leb* meaning "the heart; also used (figuratively) very widely for the feelings, the will and even the intellect; likewise for the centre of anything…" Only God knows the roots of mental strongholds that are residing within us. No one (psychiatrist or counselor) and nothing (pain medication, alcohol, drugs, etc.) can remove those things from us. It's only through Jesus Christ that we can be free! The Lord works through His body, members of the body of Christ who are mature in Him, to assist in one's healing process through listening and healing prayer as one bares one's heart in confidence. It is written in James 5:16 – *"Confess your faults one to another, and pray one for another, that ye may be healed. The effectual fervent prayer of a righteous man availeth much."* Christ was made to be sin for us as He received our carnal nature in His own Self on the cross. As we give Him our cares and anxieties, our carnal acts and idolatrous sins, our unhealthy expressions of anger, rage, bad feelings toward others, etc., He receives them because He redeemed us by His own blood! Our carnal nature, the old man, is His. Give it to Him and continue to renew your mind to His truths. Enjoy His presence through oneness with Him and walk in newness of life that you may be a light to others. Hallelujah!

> *For the word of God is living and powerful, and sharper than any two-edged sword, piercing even to the division of soul and spirit, and of joints and marrow, and is a discerner of the thoughts and intents of the heart. And there is no creature hidden from His sight, but all things are naked and open to the eyes of Him to whom we must give account. Seeing then that we have a great High Priest who has passed through the heavens, Jesus the Son of God, let us hold fast our confession. For we do not have a High Priest who cannot sympathize with our weaknesses, but was in all points tempted as we are, yet without sin. Let us therefore come boldly to the throne of grace, that we may obtain mercy and find grace to help in time of need.*
>
> (Hebrews 4:12-16, NKJV)

Jesus perfectly pleased His Father in every way and <u>mastered</u> sin for us through His obedience in going to the cross (2 Corinthians 5:21). We are now in Him, in His righteousness and in His victory (Acts 17:28; Romans 12:1-2; Ephesians 4:22-24; 1 John 5:4)! Paul said in Romans 8:6 – <u>*"For to be carnally minded is death; but to be spiritually minded is life and peace."*</u> As stated above in Hebrews 4:12, as the *spirit of the mind* or *inmost mind* is renewed to the truth of God's Word concerning the new man, it helps us to discern properly the old man, our carnal nature, working within us (see the **Personalized Scripture Guide – Details and Directives**, Chapter 4).

Your heavenly Father's desire is for His Word and His promises to become a reality within you. For example: Hebrews 13:5 (NKJV) – *"...For He Himself has said, 'I will never leave you nor forsake you.'"* This promise is not given when you do everything right or perfect, it's given because of His great love for you and because of what Jesus did for you in His obedience to die on the cross. He has given us His Spirit and therefore we are not alone in our quest to put to death the old man and to walk in newness of life in Him. I want to encourage you to be real with Jesus, your heavenly Father, and His Holy Spirit regarding issues of the heart. This includes situations and/or circumstances that have triggered thought patterns from the old man (e.g., feelings/emotions of fear and/or rejection, self-hatred, a deep sense of insecurity, the fear of man [e.g., their opinions], feelings of inadequacy, intimidations, wounding or wrong mindsets that can cause unhealthy expressions of anger, rage, bad feelings toward others, or idolatrous behavior). These patterns can possibly find their origin during our formative years when carnal core beliefs about self and others were formed and where family dynamics produced fear, wounding, and/or rejection—holding us captive to the old man (see **My Story – Part One**, Chapter 2). An example of this is found in Genesis 4:3-16 (AMPCE). In verse 6, the Lord asked Cain, *"Why are you angry? And why do you look sad and depressed and dejected?"* The Lord knew why Cain was angry. He wanted Cain to talk to Him about the situation in order to help Cain overcome his feelings of rejection and anger. As you see in verse 7 the Lord said, *"If you do well, will you not be accepted? And if you do not do well, sin crouches at your door; its desire is for you, but you must master it."* Evidently, there was a core belief operating in Cain that triggered this anger toward his brother, Abel. Sadly, Cain chose not to work through his feelings with the Lord but instead acted out of those feelings and killed his brother!

A very important way to master sin and/or strongholds in our own lives is to continue reinforcing the truth of God's Word within us and to be honest with the Lord concerning troubling or irrational thoughts/feelings/behavior. Otherwise, they can hold us captive to the old man and can build within us and like a volcano erupt onto others. Journaling to the Lord helps us to stay focused and be specific about situations and/or circumstances that have triggered any ungodly behavior or thought patterns. As we choose to be real with Him, He is faithful to reveal anything that is holding us captive (e.g., judgments, strongholds). Here is an example in my own life that took place in 2018:

> One Saturday afternoon, Don and I, and our grown children, Jonathan and Jessica, had planned to go to Piedmont Park to walk and enjoy the

day together. We had just finished lunch and I was at the kitchen sink washing up a few dishes and thinking that we were about ready to leave for the park, when Don said he wanted to do something before we left. Immediately, after he said that, bad feelings and ungodly thoughts about him began to erupt within me. I did not direct those thoughts and feelings toward him but was very concerned as to where they were coming from. It was like they were coming from a place that I had no control over. The next day I journaled my concern to the Lord, journaling what took place and confessing to the Lord how sorry I was about my bad feelings and ungodly thoughts toward Don. Afterwards, I went about my day and later that afternoon, as I was going into the kitchen, the Lord spoke to me and said, "This came from an existing judgment." The next morning I began again, journaling to the Lord, asking Him to please reveal the judgment in me that caused those bad feelings and ungodly thoughts to erupt. Two days later, He opened me up to see the judgment. He revealed to me that as a child, I had judged my mother of being hateful and selfish. As a child, I knew my mom loved me and my sister (e.g., a stay-at-home mom, prepared our meals, kept a clean environment in our home, rarely left us with a babysitter, did not drink alcohol or partake in other drugs). However, throughout my childhood, there were many times when I saw her as hateful and selfish (e.g., she was hard to please, had the final say in our home, and at times her behavior was harsh). But I never thought of it as a judgment; therefore, I never repented of it nor renounced it. When the Lord revealed this to me, I went out on the sunporch where I do most of my praying, got on my knees, and began to weep deeply before Him in true repentance. A couple of weeks later, I went to Don and told him what had happened and the harsh judgment that had formed within me. I asked him to forgive me for including him in that judgment and he graciously did.

As the Lord shined light into this dark place within my heart, I repented and I am now free from this judgment! The Lord also helped me to see that most judgments concerning myself and/or others stemmed from my childhood (e.g., comparing myself to others, the influence of home life and social interaction, how I internalized behavior patterns from significant others). I felt this example important to share with you in order for you to see the importance of being real with the Lord. Jesus said in Matthew 7:1-2, *"Judge not, that ye be not judged. For with what judgment ye judge, ye shall be judged: and with what measure ye mete, it shall be measured to you again."* What exactly does that mean? Just imagine, for a moment, if over the years I had not been renewing my mind to God's Word and if years prior the protective covering had not been removed from me and this had taken place. The result could have been much worse. The bad feelings and ungodly thoughts that erupted on the inside of me toward my husband, could have easily erupted onto him in front of our children, revealing to them and to Don that I was hateful and selfish because I was not getting what I wanted (*…and with what measure ye mete, it shall be measured to you again*)!

David was the apple of God's eye and so are we who are in Christ (Psalm 17:8; Zechariah 2:1-10). I believe portions of the book of Psalms contain much of David's prayer journal. He poured out his heart before the Lord (Psalm 142:2). Below are examples:

- Psalm 3 – When he fled from his son, Absalom.
- Psalm 35 and 41 – Concerning his enemies.
- Psalm 51 – When Nathan the prophet went to him, concerning his relationship with Bathsheba.
- Psalm 56 – When the Philistines captured him in Gath.
- Psalm 57 – When he fled from Saul into the cave.
- Psalm 63 – When he was in the wilderness of Judah.

And in Psalm 62:8, David told us to pour out our hearts before the Lord, *"Trust in him at all times; ye people, pour out your heart before him: God is a refuge for us."* The Lord did not intend for us to be independent from Him. Since He created Adam and Eve, before the fall, His plan and purpose has not changed. He never changes (Malachi 3:6; Hebrews 13:8). His desire is for us to put off the old man and for Christ's character and nature to be resident and flowing from within us as we put on the new man. I also believe you will find your journaling to become less and less as strongholds and judgments are removed and as your inner man becomes stronger in Him, rooted and grounded in His love (Ephesians 3:14-19). Journaling helps us get to the heart of the matter with the Lord, as He is our Wonderful Counselor! (Isaiah 9:6-AMPCE).

In closing, I would like to share how my husband, Don, described journaling:

> One day Don and I were sitting outside on our front porch talking about the Lord and we began talking about the importance of journaling to Him and Don said, "Journaling is like taking a bucket and

lowering it down into the well of your heart, the deep recesses of your being—drawing up things like bitterness, resentment, fears, insecurities, pain, worries, and cares that hold you captive to the old man—and pouring it out before Him."

Instructions:

This prayer journal is divided into three sections as outlined below. Each section includes five copies. You are welcome to make additional copies, or use your own journal:

Part One – Beginning with thanksgiving, Part One is designed for you to cast all your cares, concerns, and fears (e.g., anxieties, worries, frustrations, disappointments, intimidations) upon your heavenly Father who cares for you (Mark 4:7, 14, 18-19; 1 Peter 5:6-7). If you feel that any of these have become too difficult to overcome, it is important to be specific and real (honest) with the Lord by going to Part Three.

Part Two – Beginning with thanksgiving, Part Two is designed to help you work through any worldly addictions or idolatrous or fleshly sin(s) of the old man (e.g., the love for money, fame, gluttony, substance abuse, pornography, sex outside of God's design for marriage, emotional dependency, control, manipulation – Mark 4:7, 14, 18-19; Matthew 6:24; Philippians 3:18-19). This helps you to acknowledge wrong behavior as sin through repentance (acknowledging the behavior as sin, asking the Lord for forgiveness and to help you, by His grace, to turn from that old man to the new man in Christ – 1 John 1:7-9; Ephesians 5:25-27). Otherwise, unrepented sin can open the door to demonic oppression, which can have a strong influence over your thoughts, feelings, and actions. If you feel that any sins you have listed have become strongholds in your life and difficult to overcome, it is important to be specific and honest with the Lord by going to Part Three.

Part Three – Beginning with thanksgiving, Part Three is designed for you to be honest with your heavenly Father concerning situations, circumstances, and interactions with another that caused issues of the heart to arise which hinder you from living out of the new man, such as: feelings/emotions of fear and/or rejection, self-hatred, a deep sense of insecurity, feelings of inadequacy, intimidations, the fear of man (e.g., their opinions), wounding or wrong mindsets that can cause unhealthy expressions of anger, rage, bad feelings toward others, and idolatrous behavior. Again, these fears/mindsets/strongholds/judgments can possibly find their origin during our formative years when carnal core beliefs about self and others were formed and where family dynamics produced fear, wounding, and/or rejection that holds us captive to the old man.

After being real with the Lord concerning the particular situation, circumstance, or interaction with another that caused these feelings/emotions to arise, I highly recommend that you prayerfully consider having an accountability partner, a mature Christian, who can help you walk through any areas of difficulty. Confessing your faults to another, after having confessed them to the Lord, will help you work through some of these difficult areas as you bring them to the light and receive healing prayer, as well as hearing someone reinforce the truth of God's Word into your life (James 5:16) – for an example, please read **A Testimony**, Exhibit D. Also, you may want to consider attending a healing ministry like a *Living Waters Program* and/or Christian counseling in order to bring you into an environment for the Lord to heal any wounding and/or bring to light any strongholds or root issues (e.g., core beliefs and mindsets about yourself and others that formed and/or wounding that occurred during your formative years that holds you captive to the old man). Confession, forgiveness, and healing prayer with mature believers in Christ helps to bring healing to your heart and soul (James 5:16). Please see **Support and Help**.

Let's look again at a portion of Scripture that we looked at earlier:

> *Seeing then that we have a great High Priest who has passed through the heavens, Jesus the Son of God, let us hold fast our confession. <u>For we do not have a High Priest who cannot sympathize with our weaknesses, but was in all points tempted as we are, yet without sin. Let us therefore come boldly to the throne of grace, that we may obtain mercy and find grace to help in time of need.</u>*
>
> (Hebrews 4:14-16, NKJV)

As we bring our pain to Him, Jesus does sympathize with us and He provides mercy and grace to help us in our time of need. He is faithful and He is our Wonderful Counselor! (Isaiah 9:6-AMPCE).

This prayer journal is for your benefit and of course, is optional as you may choose to pour your heart out to the Lord by putting your fingers to the keyboard, using a notebook, or verbally talking to Him. The key is to be honest with Him in whatever manner works best for you.

Even though journaling to the Lord is optional, below are six reasons why writing is valuable and, I believe, worthwhile:

1. **Helps you to stay focused.** It is difficult to write and think of other things at the same time. Therefore, expressing your heart through writing helps you get to the heart of the matter with the Lord and with yourself as you lay it out before Him.

2. **Detailed.** It helps you to be specific regarding angry or hurt feelings or thought patterns that hold you captive to the old man, your carnal nature (Psalm 62:8; 142:2).

3. **Keeps you real with yourself, God, and others.** Instead of acting out of the old man, it is important to share with the Lord and release to Him situations/circumstances or interactions with others that arouse angry/hurt feelings or thought patterns that are holding you captive to the old man. As you are real with the Lord, it also helps to form a bond of intimacy with Him, producing a greater level of confidence knowing that He has the fear, the care, the worry, the anxiety, etc. At the same time, it is essential to have a fresh mental and spiritual attitude by continuing to plant and water His Words of truth in your heart and mind, as it relates to the new man (see the ***Personalized Scripture Guide – Details and Directives***, Chapter 4). As you continue to do this, the Lord is faithful to bring up areas that need to go to the cross in order for the new man in Christ to become more of a reality within you (Ephesians 4:20-24).

4. **Helps establish true relationship** with the Lord and dependence upon Him.

5. **Helps to remove weeds/thorn plants** (i.e., cares and anxieties of the world, deceitfulness of riches, and the craving and passionate desire for other things) and hard places (e.g., bitterness, resentment, judgments, ungodly beliefs, pain/wounding, unconfessed sin which produces rebellion) from your heart (Mark 4:5-7, 14, 16-19 – AMPCE).

6. **Helps to keep you from speaking non-productive words** (Matthew 12:36-37).

Remember, journaling helps us get to the heart of the matter with the Lord!

PRAYER JOURNAL - PART ONE

DESIGNED TO HELP PUT OFF THE OLD MAN CONCERNING:

- **Cares and Anxieties of this World and Distractions of the Age (thorn plants that choke the Word and It becomes unfruitful)**

Note: There have been many times when I would begin to jot down, as bullet points, things I was dreading, fears I was dealing with, or cares and concerns of the day (e.g., 1. our finances, 2. my eating habits, 3. cleaning the house, 4. going on a trip), when other things I was unaware of would begin to surface. So, instead of a list of five or six cares or concerns going to the Lord, it would grow into fifteen or twenty.

Date: _____

"Dear Lord Jesus, Father God, Holy Spirit:

I will enter Your gates with thanksgiving, and into Your courts with praise (Psalm 100:4-5). Thank You for Your goodness. Thank You for Your mercies that are new every morning. Thank You for Your grace that is sufficient. Thank You for Your peace that passes all understanding. Thank You for Your presence. Thank You for Your faithfulness and for Your longsuffering toward me. Thank You for Your wisdom. Thank You for Your truth that dispels darkness. Thank You for Your comforts… You are worthy of worship, praise, honor, and thanks!

Lord, I choose to cast all of my cares, including any fears or concerns, upon You because You care for me (1 Peter 5:7). Thank You for receiving these cares, as I know You care for me."

Now begin to cast all of your cares, concerns, or fears (e.g., anxieties, insecurities, worries, disappointments, intimidations, disappointments, frustrations). As you write down the ones you know, more may follow. <u>If you need more space, please use the back of this sheet or notebook paper.</u> If you feel you need to pour your heart out to the Lord with specifics concerning any of these you list go to Part Three (for an example, see Exhibit C).

1. _____ 10. _____
2. _____ 11. _____
3. _____ 12. _____
4. _____ 13. _____
5. _____ 14. _____
6. _____ 15. _____
7. _____ 16. _____
8. _____ 17. _____
9. _____ 18. _____

"You will guard him and keep him in constant peace whose mind [both its inclination and its character] is stayed on You, because he commits himself to You, leans on You, and hopes confidently in You" (Isaiah 26:3) - AMPCE.

Note: If you feel that any of these cares, concerns, or fears have become too difficult to overcome, it is important to be specific and real (honest) with the Lord by going to Part Three.

Date: _____

"Dear Lord Jesus, Father God, Holy Spirit:

I will enter Your gates with thanksgiving, and into Your courts with praise (Psalm 100:4-5). Thank You for Your goodness. Thank You for Your mercies that are new every morning. Thank You for Your grace that is sufficient. Thank You for Your peace that passes all understanding. Thank You for Your presence. Thank You for Your faithfulness and for Your longsuffering toward me. Thank You for Your wisdom. Thank You for Your truth that dispels darkness. Thank You for Your comforts… You are worthy of worship, praise, honor, and thanks!

Lord, I choose to cast all of my cares, including any fears or concerns, upon You because You care for me (1 Peter 5:7). Thank You for receiving these cares, as I know You care for me."

Now begin to cast all of your cares, concerns, or fears (e.g., anxieties, insecurities, worries, disappointments, intimidations, disappointments, frustrations). As you write down the ones you know, more may follow. <u>If you need more space, please use the back of this sheet or notebook paper.</u> If you feel you need to pour your heart out to the Lord with specifics concerning any of these you list go to Part Three (for an example, see Exhibit C).

1. _____   10. _____
2. _____   11. _____
3. _____   12. _____
4. _____   13. _____
5. _____   14. _____
6. _____   15. _____
7. _____   16. _____
8. _____   17. _____
9. _____   18. _____

"You will guard him and keep him in constant peace whose mind [both its inclination and its character] is stayed on You, because he commits himself to You, leans on You, and hopes confidently in You" (Isaiah 26:3) - AMPCE.

Note: If you feel that any of these cares, concerns, or fears have become too difficult to overcome, it is important to be specific and real (honest) with the Lord by going to Part Three.

Date: _____

"Dear Lord Jesus, Father God, Holy Spirit:

I will enter Your gates with thanksgiving, and into Your courts with praise (Psalm 100:4-5). Thank You for Your goodness. Thank You for Your mercies that are new every morning. Thank You for Your grace that is sufficient. Thank You for Your peace that passes all understanding. Thank You for Your presence. Thank You for Your faithfulness and for Your longsuffering toward me. Thank You for Your wisdom. Thank You for Your truth that dispels darkness. Thank You for Your comforts… You are worthy of worship, praise, honor, and thanks!

Lord, I choose to cast all of my cares, including any fears or concerns, upon You because You care for me (1 Peter 5:7). Thank You for receiving these cares, as I know You care for me."

Now begin to cast all of your cares, concerns, or fears (e.g., anxieties, insecurities, worries, disappointments, intimidations, disappointments, frustrations). As you write down the ones you know, more may follow. <u>If you need more space, please use the back of this sheet or notebook paper.</u> If you feel you need to pour your heart out to the Lord with specifics concerning any of these you list go to Part Three (for an example, see Exhibit C).

1. _____
2. _____
3. _____
4. _____
5. _____
6. _____
7. _____
8. _____
9. _____
10. _____
11. _____
12. _____
13. _____
14. _____
15. _____
16. _____
17. _____
18. _____

"You will guard him and keep him in constant peace whose mind [both its inclination and its character] is stayed on You, because he commits himself to You, leans on You, and hopes confidently in You" (Isaiah 26:3) - AMPCE.

Note: If you feel that any of these cares, concerns, or fears have become too difficult to overcome, it is important to be specific and real (honest) with the Lord by going to Part Three.

Date: _____

"Dear Lord Jesus, Father God, Holy Spirit:

I will enter Your gates with thanksgiving, and into Your courts with praise (Psalm 100:4-5). Thank You for Your goodness. Thank You for Your mercies that are new every morning. Thank You for Your grace that is sufficient. Thank You for Your peace that passes all understanding. Thank You for Your presence. Thank You for Your faithfulness and for Your longsuffering toward me. Thank You for Your wisdom. Thank You for Your truth that dispels darkness. Thank You for Your comforts… You are worthy of worship, praise, honor, and thanks!

Lord, I choose to cast all of my cares, including any fears or concerns, upon You because You care for me (1 Peter 5:7). Thank You for receiving these cares, as I know You care for me."

Now begin to cast all of your cares, concerns, or fears (e.g., anxieties, insecurities, worries, disappointments, intimidations, disappointments, frustrations). As you write down the ones you know, more may follow. <u>If you need more space, please use the back of this sheet or notebook paper.</u> If you feel you need to pour your heart out to the Lord with specifics concerning any of these you list go to Part Three (for an example, see Exhibit C).

1. _____	10. _____
2. _____	11. _____
3. _____	12. _____
4. _____	13. _____
5. _____	14. _____
6. _____	15. _____
7. _____	16. _____
8. _____	17. _____
9. _____	18. _____

"You will guard him and keep him in constant peace whose mind [both its inclination and its character] is stayed on You, because he commits himself to You, leans on You, and hopes confidently in You" (Isaiah 26:3) - AMPCE.

Note: If you feel that any of these cares, concerns, or fears have become too difficult to overcome, it is important to be specific and real (honest) with the Lord by going to Part Three.

Date: _____

"Dear Lord Jesus, Father God, Holy Spirit:

I will enter Your gates with thanksgiving, and into Your courts with praise (Psalm 100:4-5). Thank You for Your goodness. Thank You for Your mercies that are new every morning. Thank You for Your grace that is sufficient. Thank You for Your peace that passes all understanding. Thank You for Your presence. Thank You for Your faithfulness and for Your longsuffering toward me. Thank You for Your wisdom. Thank You for Your truth that dispels darkness. Thank You for Your comforts… You are worthy of worship, praise, honor, and thanks!

Lord, I choose to cast all of my cares, including any fears or concerns, upon You because You care for me (1 Peter 5:7). Thank You for receiving these cares, as I know You care for me."

Now begin to cast all of your cares, concerns, or fears (e.g., anxieties, insecurities, worries, disappointments, intimidations, disappointments, frustrations). As you write down the ones you know, more may follow. <u>If you need more space, please use the back of this sheet or notebook paper.</u> If you feel you need to pour your heart out to the Lord with specifics concerning any of these you list go to Part Three (for an example, see Exhibit C):

1. _____
2. _____
3. _____
4. _____
5. _____
6. _____
7. _____
8. _____
9. _____
10. _____
11. _____
12. _____
13. _____
14. _____
15. _____
16. _____
17. _____
18. _____

"You will guard him and keep him in constant peace whose mind [both its inclination and its character] is stayed on You, because he commits himself to You, leans on You, and hopes confidently in You" (Isaiah 26:3) - AMPCE.

Note: If you feel that any of these cares, concerns, or fears have become too difficult to overcome, it is important to be specific and real (honest) with the Lord by going to Part Three.

PRAYER JOURNAL - PART TWO

DESIGNED TO HELP PUT OFF THE OLD MAN CONCERNING:

- **False Glamour, Deceitfulness of Riches, and the Craving and Passionate Desire for Other Things**

Notes:
1. If you feel that any of the sins you list in Part Two have become difficult for you to overcome you would then go to Part Three in order to be specific and real with the Lord (i.e., journaling the specific circumstance or situation and the specific thought process that would draw you to go after others and/or things to meet your needs rather than Christ). After being honest with Him, I recommend that you prayerfully consider an accountability partner, a mature Christian, who can help you walk through any areas of difficulty. Confessing your faults to another, <u>after having confessed them to the Lord</u>, will help you work through some of these areas in your life as you bring them to the light and receive prayer, as well as hearing someone reinforce the truth of God's Word in your life (James 5:16).

2. If you are having difficulty overcoming aspects of your carnal nature, you may want to attend a healing ministry like a Living Waters Program and/or Christian counseling in order to bring you into an environment for the Lord to heal any wounding and/or bring to light any strongholds or root issues (e.g., carnal core beliefs about yourself and others that formed and/or wounding that occurred during your formative years that keeps you bound to the old man). Confession, forgiveness, and healing prayers with mature believers in Christ helps to bring healing to your heart and soul (James 5:16). Please see **Support and Help**.

Date: _____

"Dear Lord Jesus, Father God, Holy Spirit:

I will enter Your gates with thanksgiving, and into Your courts with praise (Psalm 100:4-5). Thank You for Your goodness. Thank You for Your mercies that are new every morning. Thank You for Your grace that is sufficient. Thank You for Your peace that passes all understanding. Thank You for Your presence. Thank You for Your faithfulness and for Your longsuffering toward me. Thank You for Your wisdom. Thank You for Your truth that dispels darkness. Thank You for Your comforts… You are worthy of worship, praise, honor, and thanks!

Lord, I need Your help in order to be free from the strong cravings and desires that keep me captive to sin. I confess to You the following idolatrous and/or fleshly sin(s) of the old man *(e.g., the love for money and/or fame, gluttony, substance abuse, pornography, sex outside of God's design for marriage, emotional dependency, control, manipulation, covetousness)*:

_____
_____
_____
_____
_____
_____

Lord, I ask You to forgive me and to cleanse me from all unrighteousness. You are my Advocate with the Father, and the atoning sacrifice for my sins (1 John 2:1-2). I receive Your forgiveness and cleansing (1 John 4:15). Thank you for the abundance of Your grace and the gift of righteousness to reign in this life in Christ Jesus (Romans 5:17). I choose to set my mind and keep it set on things above as You are the only One that can fill the deep longings of my heart. Thank You for Your grace to help me and strengthen me to be an overcomer." *(If your sin included someone [e.g., sexual and/or emotional dependency], I want to encourage you to ask the Lord if you should go to that person and ask them to forgive you as well).*

Note: If you feel that any sins you have listed have become strongholds in your life and therefore difficult to overcome, it is important to be specific and honest with the Lord by going to Part Three.

Date: _____

"Dear Lord Jesus, Father God, Holy Spirit:

I will enter Your gates with thanksgiving, and into Your courts with praise (Psalm 100:4-5). Thank You for Your goodness. Thank You for Your mercies that are new every morning. Thank You for Your grace that is sufficient. Thank You for Your peace that passes all understanding. Thank You for Your presence. Thank You for Your faithfulness and for Your longsuffering toward me. Thank You for Your wisdom. Thank You for Your truth that dispels darkness. Thank You for Your comforts… You are worthy of worship, praise, honor, and thanks!

Lord, I need Your help in order to be free from the strong cravings and desires that keep me captive to sin. I confess to You the following idolatrous and/or fleshly sin(s) of the old man *(e.g., the love for money and/or fame, gluttony, substance abuse, pornography, sex outside of God's design for marriage, emotional dependency, control, manipulation, covetousness)*:

_____
_____
_____
_____
_____
_____

Lord, I ask You to forgive me and to cleanse me from all unrighteousness. You are my Advocate with the Father, and the atoning sacrifice for my sins (1 John 2:1-2). I receive Your forgiveness and cleansing (1 John 4:15). Thank you for the abundance of Your grace and the gift of righteousness to reign in this life in Christ Jesus (Romans 5:17). I choose to set my mind and keep it set on things above as You are the only One that can fill the deep longings of my heart. Thank You for Your grace to help me and strengthen me to be an overcomer." *(If your sin included someone [e.g., sexual and/or emotional dependency], I want to encourage you to ask the Lord if you should go to that person and ask them to forgive you as well).*

Note: If you feel that any sins you have listed have become strongholds in your life and therefore difficult to overcome, it is important to be specific and honest with the Lord by going to Part Three.

Date: _____

"Dear Lord Jesus, Father God, Holy Spirit:

I will enter Your gates with thanksgiving, and into Your courts with praise (Psalm 100:4-5). Thank You for Your goodness. Thank You for Your mercies that are new every morning. Thank You for Your grace that is sufficient. Thank You for Your peace that passes all understanding. Thank You for Your presence. Thank You for Your faithfulness and for Your longsuffering toward me. Thank You for Your wisdom. Thank You for Your truth that dispels darkness. Thank You for Your comforts… You are worthy of worship, praise, honor, and thanks!

Lord, I need Your help in order to be free from the strong cravings and desires that keep me captive to sin. I confess to You the following idolatrous and/or fleshly sin(s) of the old man *(e.g., the love for money and/or fame, gluttony, substance abuse, pornography, sex outside of God's design for marriage, emotional dependency, control, manipulation, covetousness)*:

_____
_____
_____
_____
_____
_____

Lord, I ask You to forgive me and to cleanse me from all unrighteousness. You are my Advocate with the Father, and the atoning sacrifice for my sins (1 John 2:1-2). I receive Your forgiveness and cleansing (1 John 4:15). Thank you for the abundance of Your grace and the gift of righteousness to reign in this life in Christ Jesus (Romans 5:17). I choose to set my mind and keep it set on things above as You are the only One that can fill the deep longings of my heart. Thank You for Your grace to help me and strengthen me to be an overcomer." *(If your sin included someone [e.g., sexual and/or emotional dependency], I want to encourage you to ask the Lord if you should go to that person and ask them to forgive you as well).*

Note: If you feel that any sins you have listed have become strongholds in your life and therefore difficult to overcome, it is important to be specific and honest with the Lord by going to Part Three.

Date: _____

"Dear Lord Jesus, Father God, Holy Spirit:

I will enter Your gates with thanksgiving, and into Your courts with praise (Psalm 100:4-5). Thank You for Your goodness. Thank You for Your mercies that are new every morning. Thank You for Your grace that is sufficient. Thank You for Your peace that passes all understanding. Thank You for Your presence. Thank You for Your faithfulness and for Your longsuffering toward me. Thank You for Your wisdom. Thank You for Your truth that dispels darkness. Thank You for Your comforts… You are worthy of worship, praise, honor, and thanks!

Lord, I need Your help in order to be free from the strong cravings and desires that keep me captive to sin. I confess to You the following idolatrous and/or fleshly sin(s) of the old man *(e.g., the love for money and/or fame, gluttony, substance abuse, pornography, sex outside of God's design for marriage, emotional dependency, control, manipulation, covetousness)*:

_____
_____
_____
_____
_____
_____

Lord, I ask You to forgive me and to cleanse me from all unrighteousness. You are my Advocate with the Father, and the atoning sacrifice for my sins (1 John 2:1-2). I receive Your forgiveness and cleansing (1 John 4:15). Thank you for the abundance of Your grace and the gift of righteousness to reign in this life in Christ Jesus (Romans 5:17). I choose to set my mind and keep it set on things above as You are the only One that can fill the deep longings of my heart. Thank You for Your grace to help me and strengthen me to be an overcomer." *(If your sin included someone [e.g., sexual and/or emotional dependency], I want to encourage you to ask the Lord if you should go to that person and ask them to forgive you as well).*

Note: If you feel that any sins you have listed have become strongholds in your life and therefore difficult to overcome, it is important to be specific and honest with the Lord by going to Part Three.

Date: _____

"Dear Lord Jesus, Father God, Holy Spirit:

I will enter Your gates with thanksgiving, and into Your courts with praise (Psalm 100:4-5). Thank You for Your goodness. Thank You for Your mercies that are new every morning. Thank You for Your grace that is sufficient. Thank You for Your peace that passes all understanding. Thank You for Your presence. Thank You for Your faithfulness and for Your longsuffering toward me. Thank You for Your wisdom. Thank You for Your truth that dispels darkness. Thank You for Your comforts… You are worthy of worship, praise, honor, and thanks!

Lord, I need Your help in order to be free from the strong cravings and desires that keep me captive to sin. I confess to You the following idolatrous and/or fleshly sin(s) of the old man *(e.g., the love for money and/or fame, gluttony, substance abuse, pornography, sex outside of God's design for marriage, emotional dependency, control, manipulation, covetousness)*:

_____
_____
_____
_____
_____
_____

Lord, I ask You to forgive me and to cleanse me from all unrighteousness. You are my Advocate with the Father, and the atoning sacrifice for my sins (1 John 2:1-2). I receive Your forgiveness and cleansing (1 John 4:15). Thank you for the abundance of Your grace and the gift of righteousness to reign in this life in Christ Jesus (Romans 5:17). I choose to set my mind and keep it set on things above as You are the only One that can fill the deep longings of my heart. Thank You for Your grace to help me and strengthen me to be an overcomer." *(If your sin included someone [e.g., sexual and/or emotional dependency], I want to encourage you to ask the Lord if you should go to that person and ask them to forgive you as well).*

Note: If you feel that any sins you have listed have become strongholds in your life and therefore difficult to overcome, it is important to be specific and honest with the Lord by going to Part Three.

PRAYER JOURNAL PART THREE

DESIGNED TO HELP PUT OFF THE OLD MAN CONCERNING:

- **Behavior Patterns and Mindsets**

Notes:
1. Anger is a God-given emotion and needs to be controlled by the nature of Christ in us (Colossians 1:27). Paul said in Ephesians 4:26, "Be ye angry, and sin not: let not the sun go down on your wrath."

*2. Anger can be a manifestation of control and manipulation and/or a stronghold of pride and/or insecurity. It can also be attributed to pain or unmet needs, where core beliefs and mindsets formed and/or wounding occurred during your formative years—holding you captive to the old man—the carnal nature. If you feel anger has control of you rather than you having control of anger, I would recommend that you prayerfully consider having an accountability partner, a mature Christian, who can help you walk through any areas of difficulty. Confessing your faults to another, <u>after having journaled them to the Lord</u>, will help you work through some of these areas in your life as you bring them to the light and receive prayer, as well as hearing someone reinforce the truth of God's Word within you (James 5:16) – for an example, please read **A Testimony**, Exhibit D. It is also important to continue to renew the spirit of your mind to the new man in Christ. I also recommend reading the book, When Good Men Get Angry by Bill Perkins.*

*3. If you are having difficulty overcoming aspects of your carnal nature, you may want to attend a healing ministry like a Living Waters Program and/or Christian counseling in order to bring you into an environment for the Lord to heal any wounding and/or bring to light any strongholds or root issues (e.g., carnal core beliefs about yourself and others that formed and/or wounding that occurred during your formative years—holding you captive to the old man). Confession, forgiveness, and healing prayers with mature believers in Christ helps to bring healing to your heart and soul (James 5:16). Please see **Support and Help**.*

Date: _____

"Dear Lord Jesus, Father God, Holy Spirit:

I will enter Your gates with thanksgiving, and into Your courts with praise (Psalm 100:4-5). Thank You for Your goodness. Thank You for Your mercies that are new every morning. Thank You for Your grace that is sufficient. Thank You for Your peace that passes all understanding. Thank You for Your presence. Thank You for Your faithfulness and for Your longsuffering toward me. Thank You for Your wisdom. Thank You for Your truth that dispels darkness. Thank You for Your comforts… You are worthy of worship, praise, honor, and thanks!" *Now, begin to share details by being real with the Lord concerning circumstances of life or people, including yourself, who have disrupted your well-being and the feelings associated with it (e.g., anger/rage, insecurities, fears). Also, if anything you have listed in Part One or Part Two have become difficult to overcome, please share your heart. <u>If you need more space, please use notebook paper</u> (for an example, see Exhibit C):*

_____
_____
_____
_____
_____
_____
_____
_____
_____
_____
_____
_____
_____
_____
_____
_____
_____

After you have poured your heart out to the Lord, know that He has it and trust Him with it. During the day when thoughts may arise about this issue, I want to encourage you to say, "Thank you Lord, I know You have it." Ask Him to reveal any mental strongholds or insecurities that may be causing these thoughts/feelings to be aroused (2 Corinthians

10:3-6; James 3:14-16). *Use the space provided below to write down anything the Lord speaks to you. If it includes any root issue or stronghold, release that to Him and forgive where necessary.*

_____
_____
_____
_____
_____

Forgive those who hurt/angered you and ask the Lord to forgive them too (Matthew 6:12, 14-15, 18:32-35; 25:40; Colossians 3:13). *After you have dealt with this with the Lord and after a day or two, if you are still hurting or angry about the situation, you may want to call a <u>mature believer in Christ</u> in order to bare your heart and receive healing prayer as well as hearing someone reinforce the truth of God's Word in your life* (James 5:16) – *for an example, please read* **A Testimony**, *Exhibit D. I believe it is the Lord's wisdom to then offer up thanks to Him for the one who hurt or angered you.*

Where applicable pray aloud: "Father, in the name of Jesus, I ask You to forgive me for the offense or for the hurtful and/or angry thoughts that I have toward _____ and to cleanse me from all unrighteousness. I pray You would remove this and reveal to me any root cause or stronghold and remove it from me (Psalm 103:12). I choose to forgive myself, as well. Thank You, Lord, for Your faithfulness to cleanse me (1 John 1:9). I ask You also, Father, to strengthen me in my insecurities and in my weaknesses by Your grace (Luke 22:31-34; 2 Corinthians 12:9). I command all bitterness and unforgiveness to leave me in the name of Jesus! I receive Your peace and Your strength! Amen" (Luke 17:1-6).

- If you sinned in your anger by trespassing against someone, in order to bring healing and restoration to that relationship, I want to encourage you to go to the person you may have hurt or offended and ask them to forgive you as well (Matthew 5:23-24).

Note: If you are having difficulty overcoming aspects of your carnal nature, you may want to consider attending a healing ministry like a Living Waters Program and/or Christian counseling in order to bring you into an environment for the Lord to heal any wounding and/or bring to light any strongholds or root issues (e.g., carnal core beliefs about yourself and others that formed and/or wounding that may have occurred during your formative years that keeps you bound to the old man). Confession, forgiveness, and healing prayers with mature believers in Christ helps to bring healing to your heart and soul (James 5:16). *Please see* **Support and Help**.

Date: _____

"Dear Lord Jesus, Father God, Holy Spirit:

I will enter Your gates with thanksgiving, and into Your courts with praise (Psalm 100:4-5). Thank You for Your goodness. Thank You for Your mercies that are new every morning. Thank You for Your grace that is sufficient. Thank You for Your peace that passes all understanding. Thank You for Your presence. Thank You for Your faithfulness and for Your longsuffering toward me. Thank You for Your wisdom. Thank You for Your truth that dispels darkness. Thank You for Your comforts… You are worthy of worship, praise, honor, and thanks!" *Now, begin to share details by being real with the Lord concerning circumstances of life or people, including yourself, who have disrupted your well-being and the feelings associated with it (e.g., anger/rage, insecurities, fears). Also, if anything you have listed in Part One or Part Two have become difficult to overcome, please share your heart. <u>If you need more space, please use notebook paper</u> (for an example, see Exhibit C):*

_____
_____
_____
_____
_____
_____
_____
_____
_____
_____
_____
_____
_____
_____
_____
_____
_____

After you have poured your heart out to the Lord, know that He has it and trust Him with it. During the day when thoughts may arise about this issue, I want to encourage you to say, "Thank you Lord, I know You have it." Ask Him to reveal any mental strongholds or insecurities that may be causing these thoughts/feelings to be aroused (2 Corinthians

10:3-6; James 3:14-16). *Use the space provided below to write down anything the Lord speaks to you. If it includes any root issue or stronghold, release that to Him and forgive where necessary.*

_____
_____
_____
_____
_____

Forgive those who hurt/angered you and ask the Lord to forgive them too (Matthew 6:12, 14-15, 18:32-35; 25:40; Colossians 3:13). After you have dealt with this with the Lord and after a day or two, if you are still hurting or angry about the situation, you may want to call a <u>mature believer in Christ</u> in order to bare your heart and receive healing prayer as well as hearing someone reinforce the truth of God's Word in your life (James 5:16) – for an example, please read **A Testimony**, *Exhibit D. I believe it is the Lord's wisdom to then offer up thanks to Him for the one who hurt or angered you.*

Where applicable pray aloud: "Father, in the name of Jesus, I ask You to forgive me for the offense or for the hurtful and/or angry thoughts that I have toward _____ and to cleanse me from all unrighteousness. I pray You would remove this and reveal to me any root cause or stronghold and remove it from me (Psalm 103:12). I choose to forgive myself, as well. Thank You, Lord, for Your faithfulness to cleanse me (1 John 1:9). I ask You also, Father, to strengthen me in my insecurities and in my weaknesses by Your grace (Luke 22:31-34; 2 Corinthians 12:9). I command all bitterness and unforgiveness to leave me in the name of Jesus! I receive Your peace and Your strength! Amen" (Luke 17:1-6).

- If you sinned in your anger by trespassing against someone, in order to bring healing and restoration to that relationship, I want to encourage you to go to the person you may have hurt or offended and ask them to forgive you as well (Matthew 5:23-24).

Note: If you are having difficulty overcoming aspects of your carnal nature, you may want to consider attending a healing ministry like a Living Waters Program and/or Christian counseling in order to bring you into an environment for the Lord to heal any wounding and/or bring to light any strongholds or root issues (e.g., carnal core beliefs about yourself and others that formed and/or wounding that may have occurred during your formative years that keeps you bound to the old man). Confession, forgiveness, and healing prayers with mature believers in Christ helps to bring healing to your heart and soul (James 5:16). Please see **Support and Help**.

Date: _____

"Dear Lord Jesus, Father God, Holy Spirit:

I will enter Your gates with thanksgiving, and into Your courts with praise (Psalm 100:4-5). Thank You for Your goodness. Thank You for Your mercies that are new every morning. Thank You for Your grace that is sufficient. Thank You for Your peace that passes all understanding. Thank You for Your presence. Thank You for Your faithfulness and for Your longsuffering toward me. Thank You for Your wisdom. Thank You for Your truth that dispels darkness. Thank You for Your comforts… You are worthy of worship, praise, honor, and thanks!" *Now, begin to share details by being real with the Lord concerning circumstances of life or people, including yourself, who have disrupted your well-being and the feelings associated with it (e.g., anger/rage, insecurities, fears). Also, if anything you have listed in Part One or Part Two have become difficult to overcome, please share your heart. <u>If you need more space, please use notebook paper</u> (for an example, see Exhibit C):*

_____
_____
_____
_____
_____
_____
_____
_____
_____
_____
_____
_____
_____
_____
_____
_____
_____

After you have poured your heart out to the Lord, know that He has it and trust Him with it. During the day when thoughts may arise about this issue, I want to encourage you to say, "Thank you Lord, I know You have it." Ask Him to reveal any mental strongholds or insecurities that may be causing these thoughts/feelings to be aroused (2 Corinthians

10:3-6; James 3:14-16). *Use the space provided below to write down anything the Lord speaks to you. If it includes any root issue or stronghold, release that to Him and forgive where necessary.*

_____
_____
_____
_____
_____

Forgive those who hurt/angered you and ask the Lord to forgive them too (Matthew 6:12, 14-15, 18:32-35; 25:40; Colossians 3:13). *After you have dealt with this with the Lord and after a day or two, if you are still hurting or angry about the situation, you may want to call a <u>mature believer in Christ</u> in order to bare your heart and receive healing prayer as well as hearing someone reinforce the truth of God's Word in your life (James 5:16) – for an example, please read* **A Testimony**, *Exhibit D. I believe it is the Lord's wisdom to then offer up thanks to Him for the one who hurt or angered you.*

Where applicable pray aloud: "Father, in the name of Jesus, I ask You to forgive me for the offense or for the hurtful and/or angry thoughts that I have toward _____ and to cleanse me from all unrighteousness. I pray You would remove this and reveal to me any root cause or stronghold and remove it from me (Psalm 103:12). I choose to forgive myself, as well. Thank You, Lord, for Your faithfulness to cleanse me (1 John 1:9). I ask You also, Father, to strengthen me in my insecurities and in my weaknesses by Your grace (Luke 22:31-34; 2 Corinthians 12:9). I command all bitterness and unforgiveness to leave me in the name of Jesus! I receive Your peace and Your strength! Amen" (Luke 17:1-6).

- If you sinned in your anger by trespassing against someone, in order to bring healing and restoration to that relationship, I want to encourage you to go to the person you may have hurt or offended and ask them to forgive you as well (Matthew 5:23-24).

Note: If you are having difficulty overcoming aspects of your carnal nature, you may want to consider attending a healing ministry like a Living Waters Program and/or Christian counseling in order to bring you into an environment for the Lord to heal any wounding and/or bring to light any strongholds or root issues (e.g., carnal core beliefs about yourself and others that formed and/or wounding that may have occurred during your formative years that keeps you bound to the old man). Confession, forgiveness, and healing prayers with mature believers in Christ helps to bring healing to your heart and soul (James 5:16). *Please see* **Support and Help**.

Date: _____

"Dear Lord Jesus, Father God, Holy Spirit:

I will enter Your gates with thanksgiving, and into Your courts with praise (Psalm 100:4-5). Thank You for Your goodness. Thank You for Your mercies that are new every morning. Thank You for Your grace that is sufficient. Thank You for Your peace that passes all understanding. Thank You for Your presence. Thank You for Your faithfulness and for Your longsuffering toward me. Thank You for Your wisdom. Thank You for Your truth that dispels darkness. Thank You for Your comforts… You are worthy of worship, praise, honor, and thanks!" *Now, begin to share details by being real with the Lord concerning circumstances of life or people, including yourself, who have disrupted your well-being and the feelings associated with it (e.g., anger/rage, insecurities, fears). Also, if anything you have listed in Part One or Part Two have become difficult to overcome, please share your heart. <u>If you need more space, please use notebook paper</u> (for an example, see Exhibit C):*

_____
_____
_____
_____
_____
_____
_____
_____
_____
_____
_____
_____
_____
_____
_____
_____
_____
_____

After you have poured your heart out to the Lord, know that He has it and trust Him with it. During the day when thoughts may arise about this issue, I want to encourage you to say, "Thank you Lord, I know You have it." Ask Him to reveal any mental strongholds or insecurities that may be causing these thoughts/feelings to be aroused (2 Corinthians

10:3-6; James 3:14-16). *Use the space provided below to write down anything the Lord speaks to you. If it includes any root issue or stronghold, release that to Him and forgive where necessary.*

_____
_____
_____
_____
_____

Forgive those who hurt/angered you and ask the Lord to forgive them too (Matthew 6:12, 14-15, 18:32-35; 25:40; Colossians 3:13). *After you have dealt with this with the Lord and after a day or two, if you are still hurting or angry about the situation, you may want to call a <u>mature believer in Christ</u> in order to bare your heart and receive healing prayer as well as hearing someone reinforce the truth of God's Word in your life (James 5:16) – for an example, please read* **A Testimony**, *Exhibit D. I believe it is the Lord's wisdom to then offer up thanks to Him for the one who hurt or angered you.*

Where applicable pray aloud: "Father, in the name of Jesus, I ask You to forgive me for the offense or for the hurtful and/or angry thoughts that I have toward _____ and to cleanse me from all unrighteousness. I pray You would remove this and reveal to me any root cause or stronghold and remove it from me (Psalm 103:12). I choose to forgive myself, as well. Thank You, Lord, for Your faithfulness to cleanse me (1 John 1:9). I ask You also, Father, to strengthen me in my insecurities and in my weaknesses by Your grace (Luke 22:31-34; 2 Corinthians 12:9). I command all bitterness and unforgiveness to leave me in the name of Jesus! I receive Your peace and Your strength! Amen" (Luke 17:1-6).

- If you sinned in your anger by trespassing against someone, in order to bring healing and restoration to that relationship, I want to encourage you to go to the person you may have hurt or offended and ask them to forgive you as well (Matthew 5:23-24).

Note: If you are having difficulty overcoming aspects of your carnal nature, you may want to consider attending a healing ministry like a Living Waters Program and/or Christian counseling in order to bring you into an environment for the Lord to heal any wounding and/or bring to light any strongholds or root issues (e.g., carnal core beliefs about yourself and others that formed and/or wounding that may have occurred during your formative years that keeps you bound to the old man). Confession, forgiveness, and healing prayers with mature believers in Christ helps to bring healing to your heart and soul (James 5:16). Please see **Support and Help.**

Date: _____

"Dear Lord Jesus, Father God, Holy Spirit:

I will enter Your gates with thanksgiving, and into Your courts with praise (Psalm 100:4-5). Thank You for Your goodness. Thank You for Your mercies that are new every morning. Thank You for Your grace that is sufficient. Thank You for Your peace that passes all understanding. Thank You for Your presence. Thank You for Your faithfulness and for Your longsuffering toward me. Thank You for Your wisdom. Thank You for Your truth that dispels darkness. Thank You for Your comforts… You are worthy of worship, praise, honor, and thanks!" *Now, begin to share details by being real with the Lord concerning circumstances of life or people, including yourself, who have disrupted your well-being and the feelings associated with it (e.g., anger/rage, insecurities, fears). Also, if anything you have listed in Part One or Part Two have become difficult to overcome, please share your heart. <u>If you need more space, please use notebook paper</u> (for an example, see Exhibit C):*

_____
_____
_____
_____
_____
_____
_____
_____
_____
_____
_____
_____
_____
_____
_____
_____
_____

After you have poured your heart out to the Lord, know that He has it and trust Him with it. During the day when thoughts may arise about this issue, I want to encourage you to say, "Thank you Lord, I know You have it." Ask Him to reveal any mental strongholds or insecurities that may be causing these thoughts/feelings to be aroused (2 Corinthians

10:3-6; James 3:14-16). *Use the space provided below to write down anything the Lord speaks to you. If it includes any root issue or stronghold, release that to Him and forgive where necessary.*

_____
_____
_____
_____
_____

Forgive those who hurt/angered you and ask the Lord to forgive them too (Matthew 6:12, 14-15, 18:32-35; 25:40; Colossians 3:13). *After you have dealt with this with the Lord and after a day or two, if you are still hurting or angry about the situation, you may want to call a* <u>mature believer in Christ</u> *in order to bare your heart and receive healing prayer as well as hearing someone reinforce the truth of God's Word in your life* (James 5:16) – *for an example, please read* **A Testimony**, *Exhibit D. I believe it is the Lord's wisdom to then offer up thanks to Him for the one who hurt or angered you.*

Where applicable pray aloud: "Father, in the name of Jesus, I ask You to forgive me for the offense or for the hurtful and/or angry thoughts that I have toward _____ and to cleanse me from all unrighteousness. I pray You would remove this and reveal to me any root cause or stronghold and remove it from me (Psalm 103:12). I choose to forgive myself, as well. Thank You, Lord, for Your faithfulness to cleanse me (1 John 1:9). I ask You also, Father, to strengthen me in my insecurities and in my weaknesses by Your grace (Luke 22:31-34; 2 Corinthians 12:9). I command all bitterness and unforgiveness to leave me in the name of Jesus! I receive Your peace and Your strength! Amen" (Luke 17:1-6).

- If you sinned in your anger by trespassing against someone, in order to bring healing and restoration to that relationship, I want to encourage you to go to the person you may have hurt or offended and ask them to forgive you as well (Matthew 5:23-24).

Note: If you are having difficulty overcoming aspects of your carnal nature, you may want to consider attending a healing ministry like a Living Waters Program and/or Christian counseling in order to bring you into an environment for the Lord to heal any wounding and/or bring to light any strongholds or root issues (e.g., carnal core beliefs about yourself and others that formed and/or wounding that may have occurred during your formative years that keeps you bound to the old man). Confession, forgiveness, and healing prayers with mature believers in Christ helps to bring healing to your heart and soul (James 5:16). *Please see* **Support and Help**.

Chapter 6

PRAYERS OF REPENTANCE

The following pages include prayers of repentance for wives, husbands, mothers, and fathers. Please make any changes where needed, or use your own prayer to make this heartfelt to your heavenly Father. Below are two Scripture references concerning these prayers:

Wash me thoroughly from my iniquity, and cleanse me from my sin. For I acknowledge my transgressions, and my sin is always before me. Against You, You only, have I sinned, and done this evil in Your sight—that You may be found just when You speak, and blameless when You judge. Behold, I was brought forth in iniquity, and in sin my mother conceived me. Behold, You desire truth in the inward parts, and in the hidden part You will make me to know wisdom. Purge me with hyssop, and I shall be clean; wash me, and I shall be whiter than snow. Make me hear joy and gladness, that the bones You have broken may rejoice. Hide Your face from my sins, and blot out all my iniquities. Create in me a clean heart, O God, and renew a steadfast spirit within me.

(Psalm 51:2-10, NKJV)

If we say that we have fellowship with Him, and walk in darkness, we lie and do not practice the truth. But if we walk in the light as He is in the light, we have fellowship with one another, and the blood of Jesus Christ His Son cleanses us from all sin. If we say that we have no sin, we deceive ourselves, and the truth is not in us. If we confess our sins, he is faithful and just to forgive us our sins and to cleanse us from all unrighteousness. If we say that we have not sinned, we make Him a liar, and His word is not in us.

(1 John 1:6-10, NKJV)

A Prayer of Repentance Concerning:

My Responsibility as a Wife
(Fill in blanks with your husband's name)

"Father, in the name of Jesus, You are the righteous Judge, not me. I repent and ask Your forgiveness for trying to change my husband. I forgive _____ for not meeting my expectations as a husband and a father (*if applicable*). I ask You to forgive me for judging him. I lay down my expectations, and I choose to operate in faith, hope, and love toward him. I choose to put my trust in You. Forgive me for belittling him, for not respecting him, and at times, for even despising him for his actions and behavior. Cleanse me from resentment and bitterness of heart. I choose not to judge him, but to honor and serve him with all of my heart, knowing that as I serve my husband and my family, I am actually serving You. Help me to be an example of Your character and nature of what the true church, the bride of Christ, should look like. From this day forward, I choose to come to You first and pour out my heart to You, my Wonderful Counselor, concerning anything my husband may say or do that would cause me to feel unwanted, devalued, rejected, threatened, agitated, angered, disturbed, or would cause feelings of fear, which include disappointments, anxieties, worries, insecurities, or intimidations to arise within me. I choose to do this instead of taking any feelings of insecurities and fears out on my husband. Lord, Paul said in 1 Corinthians 11:3 (AMPCE), *"But I want you to know and realize that Christ is the Head of every man, the head of a woman is her husband, and the Head of Christ is God."* I choose to honor my husband as my head. You are his Head, and I trust You to work in my heart and in my husband's heart to fulfill Your plan and purpose in and through us and to be more Christlike in character. Amen (let it be so)!"

A Prayer of Repentance Concerning:

My Responsibility as a Husband
(Fill in blanks with your wife's name)

"Father, in the name of Jesus, You are the righteous Judge, not me. I repent and ask Your forgiveness for trying to change my wife. I forgive _____ for not meeting my expectations as a wife and a mother (*if applicable*). I ask You to forgive me for judging her. I lay down my expectations and I choose to operate in faith, hope, and love toward her. I choose to put my trust in You. Forgive me for belittling her, being insensitive to her, for not respecting her, and at times for even despising her for her actions and behavior. Cleanse me from all resentment and bitterness of heart. I choose not to judge her, but to honor, protect, and bless her with all of my heart, knowing that as I love my wife and my family, I am actually loving, serving, and honoring You. Help me to be an example of Your character and nature of what Christ, the Head of the church, should look like as You have placed me as head of my family. Show me how to stand in the truth in true humility and love. From this day forward, I choose to come to You first and pour out my heart to You, my Wonderful Counselor, concerning anything my wife may say or do that would cause me to feel threatened, agitated, angered, disturbed, or fear to rise within me. I choose to do this instead of taking these insecurities and fears out on her. Amen (let it be so)!"

A Prayer of Repentance Concerning:

My Responsibility as a Mother
(Fill in blanks with your child(ren)'s name and circle the applicable pronoun)

"Father, in the name of Jesus, I ask You to forgive me for the times where I have acted in an ungodly manner toward my child(ren). Forgive me for being so preoccupied with my own needs and problems that I have neglected _____ needs. From this day forward, I choose to trust You to satisfy and comfort my heart. Forgive me when I have not taken the time to listen to and to help him/her/them in his/her/their time of need. Forgive me for acting out of my anger toward _____ instead of coming to You with my pain and frustration. Forgive me for the times when I have been hard on _____ and have harassed him/her/them for not meeting my expectations. Forgive me for correcting and/or yelling at him/her/them in my anger.

Father, because of my own pain, forgive me if any of my actions or behavior has caused inner vows, judgments, bitterness, or resentment to have possibly formed in _____ heart(s). I ask You to empower me to be free from these behavior patterns that come from living out of the old man. Forgive me for the times where I have fallen short of raising _____ in the nurture and admonition of the Lord. Show me how to be consistent in my walk with You, Lord! I choose to humble myself and to be accountable not only to You but also to my husband (*if applicable*) and to my child(ren) by asking them to forgive me, as well.

Father, I also confess that at times I still act like a child. I confess that I am needy for completion in Christ. I realize that only You can bring me to a level of maturity in Christ where I operate out of Your character and nature and not out of my own insecurities, frustrations, or anger. I choose to forgive myself for the times I have acted selfishly and where my behavior toward my child(ren) has not been pleasing to You. I ask you to cleanse me from all unrighteousness and I ask for wisdom and direction for healing and proper growth in Christ for me, my husband (*if applicable*), and for my child(ren). From this day forward, I choose to humble myself before You and to be accountable to You, my husband (*if applicable*), and to my child(ren) for any acts of ungodliness toward them that may occur. Amen (let it be so)!"

Note: This applies not only to children at home, but to those who have already grown up and left the home. It is hidden sin that has not been brought to the cross that keeps us from being in right relationship with the Lord. If you are guilty of any of the following sins: emotional abuse and neglect, abandonment, sexual abuse, physical abuse, abortion, I encourage you to acknowledge that sin by confessing it to the Lord. Ask Him to forgive you and receive His cleansing and forgiveness (1 John 1:9). Afterwards, prayerfully consider confessing the sin(s) to your spouse (if applicable) or to a mature Christian and the child(ren) you sinned against, and ask for their forgiveness. These acts of repentance will help bring healing and freedom to you and to your child(ren).

A Prayer of Repentance Concerning:

My Responsibility as a Father
(Fill in blanks with your child(ren)'s name and circle the applicable pronoun)

"Father, in the name of Jesus, I ask You to forgive me for the times where I have acted in an ungodly manner toward my child(ren). Forgive me for being so preoccupied with my own needs and problems that I have neglected _____ needs. From this day forward, I choose to trust You to satisfy and comfort my heart. Forgive me when I have not taken the time to listen to and to help him/her/them in their time of need. Forgive me for acting out of my anger toward _____ instead of coming to You with my pain and frustration. Forgive me for the times when I have been hard on _____ and harassed him/her/them for not meeting my expectations. Forgive me for correcting and/or yelling at him/her/them in my anger.

Father, because of my own pain, forgive me if any of my actions or behavior has caused inner vows, judgments, bitterness, or resentment to have possibly formed in _____ heart(s). I ask You to empower me to be free from these behavior patterns that come from living out of the old man. Forgive me for the times where I have fallen short of raising _____ in the nurture and admonition of the Lord. Show me how to be consistent in my walk with You, Lord! I choose to humble myself and be accountable not only to You but also to my wife (*if applicable*) and to my children by asking them to forgive me, as well.

Father, I also confess that at times I still act like a child. I confess that I am needy for completion in Christ. I realize that only You can bring me to a level of maturity in Christ where I operate out of Your character and nature and not out of my own insecurities, frustrations, or anger. I choose to forgive myself for the times I have acted selfishly and where my behavior toward my child(ren) has not been pleasing to You. I ask you to cleanse me from all unrighteousness and I ask for wisdom and direction for healing and proper growth in Christ for me, my wife (*if applicable*), and for my child(ren). From this day forward, I choose to humble myself before You and to be accountable to You, my wife (*if applicable*), and to my child(ren) for any acts of ungodliness toward them that may occur. Amen (let it be so)!"

Note: This applies not only to children at home, but to those who have already grown up and left the home. It is hidden sin that has not been brought to the cross that keeps us from being in right relationship with the Lord. If you are guilty of any of the following sins: emotional abuse and neglect, abandonment, sexual abuse, physical abuse, abortion, I encourage you to acknowledge that sin by confessing it to the Lord. Ask Him to forgive you and receive His cleansing and forgiveness (1 John 1:9). Afterwards, prayerfully consider confessing the sin(s) to your spouse (if applicable) or to a mature Christian and the child(ren) you sinned against, and ask for their forgiveness. These acts of repentance will help bring healing and freedom to you and to your child(ren).

Chapter 7

A HEART OF THANKSGIVING
The Importance of Giving Thanks

It is important to cultivate a heart of thanksgiving and below are four Scripture references revealing the Lord's will concerning this:

1. Psalm 34:1 – *David said, <u>I will bless the LORD at all times: his praise shall continually be in my mouth</u>.*

2. Ephesians 5:18-20 – *And be not drunk with wine, wherein is excess; but be filled with the Spirit; speaking to yourselves in psalms and hymns and spiritual songs, singing and making melody in your heart to the Lord; <u>giving thanks always for all things unto God and the Father in the name of our Lord Jesus Christ</u>.*

3. 1 Thessalonians 5:18 – *<u>In everything give thanks: for this is the will of God in Christ Jesus concerning you</u>.*

4. Hebrews 13:12-15 (NKJV) – *Therefore Jesus also, that He might sanctify the people with His own blood, suffered outside the gate. Therefore let us go forth to Him, outside the camp, bearing His reproach. <u>For here we have no continuing city, but we seek the one to come. Therefore by Him let us continually offer the sacrifice of praise to God, that is, the fruit of our lips, giving thanks to His name</u>.*

Let's look at these five facts from the Bible:

- In Him we live and move and have our being (Acts 17:28).
- God will never leave us nor forsake us (Hebrews 13:5).
- Christ came to give us life and that more abundantly (John 10:10).
- We have been given all things that pertain to life and godliness (2 Peter 1:3).
- Nothing shall be able to separate us from the love of God, which is in Christ Jesus (Romans 8:38-39).

These very truths alone should cause us to want to give thanks to Him regardless of our circumstances!

Unfortunately, too many times our own self-centeredness (i.e., the cares of this world, distractions of this age, lust for other things, deceitfulness of riches) and even religious activity keeps our focus off of Him, the true meaning of life, causing our hearts to become weary and heavy laden instead of being satisfied from ourselves (Proverbs 14:14; Colossians 3:1-4). If you are bogged down with life, I want to encourage you to go to the ***Personal Prayer Journal – From your heart to His – Part One*** and list all your cares, concerns, and fears (e.g., anxieties, insecurities, worries, disappointments, intimidations, frustrations) to the Lord and ask Him to forgive you for being consumed with other things rather than Him. If need be, rededicate your life to Christ and begin to cultivate a true relationship with Him. Jesus said,

> *Come unto me, all ye that labour and are heavy laden, and I will give you rest. Take my yoke upon you, and learn of me; for I am meek and lowly in heart: and ye shall find rest unto your souls. For my yoke is easy, and my burden is light.*
>
> (Matthew 11:28-30)

The Greek word for "labour" is *kopiao*. Its meaning in the Thayer's Greek Lexicon is "to grow weary, tired, exhausted, (with toil or burdens or grief)." The Greek word for "heavy laden" is *phortizo*. Its meaning in the Thayer's Greek Lexicon is "'heavy laden' (with the burdensome requirements of the Mosaic law and of tradition, and with the consciousness of sin." In John 17:1-3, while in prayer, Jesus said, "*…And this is life eternal, that they might know thee the only true God, and Jesus Christ, whom thou has sent.*" As we set our affections on things above, the eternal things of God, we begin to understand the true meaning of life and can truly give God thanks in all things knowing that He is in control of our lives and that His love for us is great (Colossians 3:1-4; 2 Corinthians 4:18; Philippians 2:12-13; Hebrews 6:10-20, 13:20-21; 1 Peter 2:25; Ephesians 2:1-10, 3:8-21). As we continue to be single-minded, God will strengthen us and establish us in His kingdom. Peter said:

> *Humble yourselves therefore under the mighty hand of God, that he may exalt you in due time: casting all your care upon him; for he careth for you. Be sober, be vigilant; because your adversary the devil, as a roaring lion, walketh about, seeking whom he may devour: whom resist stedfast in the faith, knowing that the same afflictions are accomplished in your brethren*

that are in the world. But the God of all grace, who hath called us unto his eternal glory by Christ Jesus, after that ye have suffered a while, make you perfect, stablish, strengthen, settle you. To him be glory and dominion for ever and ever. Amen.

(1 Peter 5:6-11)

Peter also said in 1 Peter 4:19 – *"Wherefore let them that suffer according to the will of God commit the keeping of their souls to him in well doing, as unto a faithful Creator."* Paul and Silas had this revelation as they prayed and sang praises to God after they had been beaten with rods, put into an inner prison, and their feet shackled (See Acts 16:16-40 for the entire story).

We are created in God's image and in His likeness. How do you feel when you are appreciated—when your spouse, children, employer, teacher, etc., gives thanks to you for the things you've done or for who you are as a person? It certainly blesses me! On the other hand, how do you feel when you're around someone who is a complainer or seems to never be pleased? As for me, it is sad and grievous. Let's consider the children of Israel. God's intent was to bless them and to bring them into the promised land. Because they were consumed with self, and full of doubt and unbelief (they murmured and complained when things did not go their way), they all died in the wilderness and never received the promise. The only two that entered into the promised land forty years later were Caleb and Joshua who were obedient to the Lord and truly trusted in Him (Numbers 14). Jesus said in Matthew 25:40 – *"…inasmuch as ye have done it unto one of the least of these My brethren, ye have done unto Me."* When we murmur and complain to others, we murmur and complain to the Lord. Just as Moses said to the children of Israel in Exodus 16:8 (NKJV) – *"…for the LORD hears your complaints which you make against Him. And what are we? Your complaints are not against us but against the LORD."* In the same way, when we are thankful and kind toward others we are thankful and kind toward the Lord (Matthew 25:32-40). Below is an example where the Lord helped me to see the importance of giving thanks for my husband:

The Lord spoke to my heart one day when my husband, Don, and I were in the kitchen. I was sitting at the kitchen table and Don was in the kitchen doing something. I was looking at him and within myself I was picking at something that he wasn't doing right, not at that particular moment but just in his character. The Lord immediately arrested that thought and said, *"You're more focused on what he's <u>not doing</u> right than on the things <u>he does</u> do right."* I asked the Lord to forgive me and shortly after, I felt to make a list of the good qualities in my husband and I began using that list to give thanks to the Lord for him. Over the years, I have seen amazing results in my heart and changes in my husband's heart too! As we choose to make a conscious effort to give thanks, this becomes a powerful behavior pattern in our lives and helps to still the enemy's tactics in building strongholds of hate and cynicism toward others. I want to encourage you to begin to allow thanksgiving to flow from your heart toward the Lord. Thanking Him for who He is and for all that He has given you (e.g., health, hot and cold water, a roof over your head, clothing, food, provision) and also thank Him for the people in your life (e.g., your family, friends, teachers, professors). It is also important to thank Him for the body of Christ and for government officials.

In order to help you make a conscious effort to do this, along with heartfelt prayers, I have included ***A Heart of Thanksgiving Prayer Guide***. This guide is for your benefit and of course is optional. Feel free to make a copy of this prayer guide if needed. One benefit is to help you make a conscious effort to list the good things concerning your loved ones and others, and to offer up prayers for them (e.g., praying for the Lord's will to be done in their lives). It is also important to include those who you may be dealing with bitterness and resentment toward. After forgiving them and asking the Lord to forgive and to cleanse you from any wrong mindsets and attitudes toward them, begin to use this list to give thanks to the Lord for them and offer up prayers.

Please refer to the ***Scripture Guide Study Notes - Volume 2***, Note 1c and 10b for additional information and Scriptures concerning the importance of giving thanks, and Note 28b for additional information and Scriptures concerning forgiveness.

A Heart of Thanksgiving Prayer Guide

*Specifics: Again, if you are bogged down with life, I want to encourage you to go to the **Personal Prayer Journal – From your heart to His – Part One** and list all your cares, concerns, and fears (e.g., anxieties, insecurities, worries, disappointments, intimidations, frustrations) to the Lord and ask Him to forgive you for being consumed with the things of this world rather than Him. If there is any bitterness or unforgiveness toward anyone, forgive them. If you need to pour your heart out to the Lord about something or someone, I encourage you to go to the **Personal Prayer Journal – From your heart to His – Part Three** and release it to Him. Release yourself to Him so you can be a blessing to others. Then, where applicable, begin listing the good things about your individual family members and friends and use that list to give thanks to the Lord for them and pray for any needs they may have. Give thanks for and speak words of faith over the body of Christ and your local church and specific missionaries, government officials, you or your child's principal/staff/teachers/professors at school, and your supervisor/co-workers at your workplace. Give the Lord thanks for them. Thank Him for their salvation and ask for His will to be done in their lives. Let's begin by using the following thanksgiving prayer for what He has done for you and add to it:*

"Father, in the name of Jesus, thank You for who You are and for all that You have given to me. Thank You for Your provision and meeting all my needs according to Your riches in glory by Christ Jesus (Philippians 4:19). Thank You for working in me both to will and to do Your good pleasure and even in the midst of trials and hardships I choose to trust You (Philippians 2:13; Hebrews 13:20-21; 1 Thessalonians 5:18; 1 Peter 5:6-11). Thank You for Your mercies that are new every morning and for Your great faithfulness (Lamentations 3:22-23). I am mostly thankful for You, Jesus Christ, my Lord and my Savior. You gave Your life for me so that I can walk in newness of life! Thank You for food, clothing, clean water to drink, hot and cold water for bathing, a warm bed to sleep in, a roof over my head, my family, my car, my work…

_____
_____
_____
_____
_____
_____
_____

I give You thanks and offer up prayers for my family members *(insert their names and pray for their salvation [if needed] and for spiritual maturity in Christ. Pray for God's will to be done in their lives. Pray for protection, health, and for any specific needs you are aware of.)*:

My spouse/children/grandchildren:

_____
_____
_____
_____
_____

My parents/grandparents/caregivers:

_____
_____
_____
_____

My siblings/nieces/nephews/aunts/uncles/cousins:

_____
_____
_____
_____
_____

I give You thanks and offer up prayers for my friends *(insert their names and pray for their salvation [if needed] and for spiritual maturity in Christ. Pray for God's will to be done in their lives. Pray for protection, health, and for any specific needs you are aware of.)*:

_____
_____
_____
_____

I give You thanks and offer up prayers for the body of Christ and my local church. *Below is a prayer for the body of Christ. I encourage you to pray this on a regular basis:*

Father, in the name of Jesus, I pray and thank You for the body of Christ, the church.

I pray for her purity and for her maturity—that she would continue to grow in wisdom and knowledge in Christ; a bride without spot or wrinkle, that she shows forth the holiness, love, and wisdom of God. I pray the kingdom of God would be revealed in and through her. Oh Lord, be exalted in Your body. Let every member be whole and healthy in spiritual maturity. Thank You for identifying and sanctifying Your church. Thank You, Father, that Christ is glorified in His church and that she is subject to Him in all things. She has been bought with a price. Amen!

Below are areas where you can offer up specific prayers concerning your local church, your pastor, and missionaries (insert their names and pray for their spiritual maturity in Christ. Pray for God's will to be done in their lives. Pray for protection, health, and for any specific needs you are aware of.):

Local church leaders:
_____
_____
_____
_____

Brothers and sisters in Christ:
_____
_____
_____
_____

Missionaries:
_____
_____
_____
_____

"When the righteous are in authority, the people rejoice..." (Proverbs 29:2). I give You thanks and offer up prayers for the United States of America and for her elected and appointed officials and judges: president/vice-president/senators/congressional representatives/Supreme Court justices/my state and local elected and appointed officials and judges – 1 Timothy 2:1-3 *(pray for their salvation and for spiritual maturity in Christ. Pray for God's wisdom to be imparted to them to perform their duties according to His will. Pray that these officials and judges will preserve, protect, and defend the Constitution of the United States, as it was written, in order for this country to remain a*

free nation and for the preaching of the gospel of Jesus Christ and His kingdom to be able to flow freely throughout this land and the nations of the world. Pray for any other areas of concern.):

_____
_____
_____
_____

I give You thanks and offer up prayers for my school and/or my children's or grandchildren's school *(insert their names and pray for their salvation [if needed] and for spiritual maturity in Christ. Pray for God's will to be done in their lives. Pray for protection, health, and for any specific needs you are aware of.):*

Principal/staff/professors/teachers:
_____
_____
_____
_____

I give You thanks and offer up prayers for my workplace *(insert their names and pray for their salvation [if needed] and for spiritual maturity in Christ. Pray for God's will to be done in their lives. Pray for protection, health, and for any specific needs you are aware of.):*

Supervisor/co-workers:
_____
_____
_____
_____

I give You thanks and offer up prayers for *(insert their names and pray for their salvation [if needed] and for spiritual maturity in Christ. Pray for God's will to be done in their lives. Pray for protection, health, and for any specific needs you are aware of.):*

Others:
_____
_____

EXHIBITS

Exhibit A
A picture of me wearing a cowboy hat.

**Exhibit B
A portrait of me with short hair
and wearing a pretty dress.**

Exhibit C-1
An Original Prayer Journal Entry
Written

Wednesday 3/4/98

Father,
    I want to draw so close to you. This morning and yesterday evening I saw such - terrible pride - in my heart especially this morning. Don was talking about how cluttered the kitchen cabinets were - the cat food was out - there were 2 cans on the counter -- I really rubbed me the wrong way -- I told him to leave me alone, that I didn't get into his business and for him not to get into mine. But then I was cleaning and the more I thought about it the MADDER I got. I was very angry at him and I started using those terrible cuss words like a sinner who the Lord would use. Then I started thinking about the scripture that out of the abundance of the heart the mouth speaks - that's why I feel that there is hard - evil in my heart. This hasn't happened in a while. Your word says either make the tree and the fruit good or make the tree and the fruit bad. HOW? What can I do to clean out my heart Father - please help me - please forgive me

Exhibit C-2
The Original Prayer Journal Entry
Typed

Wednesday, 3/4/98

Father,

I want to draw so close to You. This morning and yesterday evening, I saw trash – terrible trash – in my heart, especially this morning. Don was talking about how cluttered the kitchen cabinets (counters) were – the cat food was out – there were two cans on the counter – – it really rubbed me the wrong way – – I told him to leave me alone that I didn't get into his business and for him not to get into mine. But then I was cleaning and the more I thought about it the MADDER I got. I was very angry at him and I started using these terrible cuss words like a sinner without the fear of the Lord would use. Then I started thinking about the Scripture that out of the abundance of the heart the mouth speaks. That's why I feel that there is trash – evil in my heart. This hasn't happened in a while. Your word says either make the tree and the fruit good or make the tree and the fruit bad. HOW? What can I do to clean out my heart Father – Please help me – please forgive me.

Scripture reference: Matthew 12:33-34

Exhibit D
A Testimony

My name is Lisa and I am Christy Morgan's niece. Christy asked me if I would prayerfully consider giving a testimony of the Lord's transforming power in my life through renewing my mind to the new man using the **_Personalized Scripture Guide_** along with being real (honest) with Him concerning my own fears and anxieties through journaling. I felt strongly to do so as I have found much strength and spiritual maturity in Him through this process. First, I think it is important to briefly share my upbringing and the stronghold of fear that I struggled with throughout my childhood and into my adult life.

As a young child I was always fearful of the Lord. I really loved the Lord, as I always wanted to please Him and my heart was always toward Him. I do not understand this because I was not raised in church but did have Christian parents, so I knew about Him and learned about Him on the rare occasions when we did go to church. At the age of four, my parents divorced, which left me and my older sister, who was seven at the time, to be raised in a split family and witnessing the struggles of a single mom. During my childhood I would pray for my parents because of my concern for them; and the rejection I felt from my dad leaving us opened the door to a spirit of fear and anxiety. At the time, I was too young to understand that it was from the enemy of my soul, Satan, who was building a stronghold of fear and anxiety within me. For example, at around the age of seven, my dad walked in the room where he saw my stepsister and me drawing stick figures doing sexual acts on a chalkboard and he scolded us for it. The rest of the evening, and even while everyone else was enjoying dinner that night, I was overtaken with fear produced by tormenting thoughts that I was going to hell. How could I have done such an evil thing, and what was going to happen to me?

Fast forward to my teenage years. I had such a fear of the Lord that it kept me from doing anything wrong. I never partied, drank alcohol, smoked a cigarette, partook in drugs, nor had sex outside of marriage. If a curse word came out of my mouth, I would immediately ask the Lord to forgive me. I had an unhealthy fear of the Lord that began to take root in me at an early age. Don't get me wrong, that fear kept me from a lot of things I shouldn't have done, but it was a condemning fear of going to hell.

Several years later, I was in my twenties and married with three small children, attending church on a regular basis, and a devoted Christian. I loved the Lord with all of my heart, but I was a mess inside. Fear and anxiety were more apparent in my life than ever before, leaving me at times paralyzed in my thinking. For example, I would cause the entire family to leave a restaurant because I had a thought that I was going to pass out and die. It was this behavior that caused my marriage to go sour because my husband didn't understand and was not supportive. Another instance was when I picked up my kids from daycare and fear gripped my soul to the point I couldn't get out of the car. It started with the same thought that I was going to pass out and die. Here I was, a mother taking care of three small children and I felt like a child myself as I was living out of my emotions and feelings. I didn't have a clue as to how to apply the Word of God in my life and I didn't know that it was such a treasure. No one had ever taught me how to walk it out. What I did know was that my Aunt Christy had been walking with the Lord and I saw Christ in her. I saw a strength in her that I wanted. So, she was my support through many of these attacks. During anxiety attacks, I would call her and she would pray with me and speak the Word over me. She would stay on the phone with me repeating the Scripture, "You have not been given a spirit of fear, but of power, love, and a sound mind." The Word of God would always destroy the thoughts that crippled me, but I couldn't do it on my own as I didn't know how.

For seven years, Christy counseled with me and I would be great for months, but it became a cycle. Fear and anxiety would rise, I would call her, she spoke life-giving words to me and prayed with me. That would hold me over until the next time. I honestly felt like a child in need of a mother, and she had become my spiritual mom. I always felt safe with her, but it wasn't her, it was the One who was at work within her. I would even pray and ask God to make me more like her because she had what I wanted. One day, in the latter part of 2003, she called me and asked if I would meet her at McDonald's as she had something to go over with me. While our kids played, she told me that the Lord showed her to give me the **Personalized Scripture Guide**, and she encouraged me to speak the Scriptures aloud 3-4 times a week, along with journaling to the Lord any tormenting fears and anxieties that arose. She also told me not to call her until I had poured my heart out to Him, and then afterwards, if I still needed to talk and to receive prayer, I could call her. This is what I needed! I needed someone to put on paper the instructions of what I needed to do! I had faith in the Word of God, but I didn't know how to make it real and get it on the inside of me. With these written instructions, I would be a fool not to discipline myself to make it a part of my life, as I needed help! My children needed a strong mother, and my husband needed a supportive wife. I followed her instructions, and every time I would get these Scriptures out and speak them out of my mouth, I felt empowered!

For six months, I renewed my mind to the new man by speaking out loud the Scriptures contained in the ***Personalized Scripture Guide*** and it became a part of who I am. After doing this spiritual exercise for six months the Word became alive within me. I can't tell you how or when. It's like a seed, and as I planted this incorruptible seed in my heart ground and continued watering the seed with the Word of God, something happened – faith began to form on the inside of me and I began to see the strength of the born-again creation become a reality within me. There were many times during the six months when speaking these Scriptures that my mind was not focused, but even so I believed in my heart it was doing something, and it was! I was becoming who I was longing to be; Christ's image was beginning to form inside of me. I was strengthened by His Words of life, and therefore, there were less calls to Christy for help and more calls of praise to Him!

In September 2006, my husband told me that he didn't love me and never did. Several weeks later, he moved out of the house and our divorce was final in May 2007. I am so thankful I had these Words of life already working on the inside of me. I did experience great hurt and rejection that pierced my soul, but I had become accustomed to taking my feelings, pain, and rejection to the Lord and being real (honest) before Him. I knew His love would come in and heal all those wounds. I also learned from speaking the Scriptures concerning work ethics and submission to authority, how to handle myself with a manager who was overbearing. During challenging times with my manager, something on the inside of me would rise up and move me to submit to authority and take my cares to the Lord. Through this process, I no longer reacted out of my emotions but gained the victory over my emotions and released them to the One who could handle it.

I am remarried now, and the Lord has restored all the enemy meant for evil. Through His Word and by His Spirit, the Lord has removed the stronghold of fear and anxiety that so tormented me. As perfect as this marriage is, there will always be trials. I am thankful for what His Word has instilled in me. I must give credit to the time and devotion I put into it and the amazing results I have seen as I've renewed my mind. I know the Father's love for me. I understand we live in a physical world, but I've learned and I am still learning that I live based on what the Word of God says, not on what I see, hear, or feel. So when trials arise in my marriage, the old me would have acted out of my feelings and addressed the issue out of my own strength, which would lead to anger, resentment, and bitterness. But now that I know who I am in Christ, and acting out of the new man, I can truly trust my Lord with all my cares and concerns. Taking these trials that arise to Him, journaling my heart to Him, releasing all the "yuck" to Him and not unloading on my husband, the Lord takes my care and supernaturally exchanges it with peace, love, and strength. I leave it with Him, and in return I show love to my husband. It's such a beautiful picture of submission.

The Word of God covers it ALL! I highly recommend **Character Development in Christ**. You will never go wrong by speaking God's Word over your life. Just like a seed that is planted and watered, the Word of God will bring forth a giant within you. It's powerful and active, and sharper than any two-edged sword. It will change your life!

Just recently, I was in a battle that included an adult child living in our home. At times, the heat was fierce and I would normally want to talk about it to others and have them add fuel to the fire. But instead, I remembered the times before when the Lord supernaturally helped me with battles, when I took my cares and concerns to Him and spoke these Scriptures in faith. So, I began to speak the Scriptures on a regular basis. I journaled and released my anger, cares, and unforgiveness to the Lord and in return, as I did this more and more each day, He gave me the grace I needed to get through this battle. I saw things come to the light that were in the dark. He gave me the ability to love and not be bitter.

I will not lie, as I was diligent about speaking the Scriptures, I noticed there was stuff coming up in me that was just ugly. While alone, I was saying things and thinking things that were so out of character. I talked to Christy about this because it concerned me that I had this in me. She reminded me that the Word was going deep within me to expose and to remove the junk coming from the old man. I knew then, I was being cleaned out. It is a constant process to be renewed. We cannot do this for a certain amount of time and think we are done and good. We are better than what we were, but we continue to get better as we continue our walk with the Lord. As soon as I feel the old man starting to rise out of me it is a clear indication that it's time to get the Scriptures out and journal, and release all that I am feeling.

I would like to add, please do not get into condemnation about how much you "do" with the ***Personalized Scripture Guide***. We all get busy and sometimes we are not able to fit this in each day. The Lord showed me to commit to do it daily, but if something comes up, it's okay. He also showed me my need to take Day Five of the *Scripture Guide* and include it along with my daily speaking of Scriptures (i.e., Day One, Day Two, Day Three, and Day Four). So, let the Holy Spirit lead and guide you as you take the time to get before Him and speak the Scriptures. Allow Him to lead you through it. I will do these for several weeks or months at a time and put it down. I will then notice I am not handling situations the way I should, and I get right back into it. Just allow Him to lead you. I have also found as I read *Heart-to-heart*, I am learning the heart of the Father. He is kind and loving and leaves me feeling safe and secure. In moments of grief and desperation, I am reminded of who He is and I find myself longing to get before Him because I know I can trust Him with everything. He has become my safe place.

Lisa Doolittle

SUPPORT AND HELP

Ministry	Resources Available
Desert Stream Ministries 706 Main Street Grandview, MO 64030	Provides help for Christians struggling with aspects of the old man or false self, regarding sexual and relational issues. Through biblical wisdom, godly support, and the power of prayer, they help Christians identify root issues of the old man and to stand in Christ as their hope and source of healing (i.e., the *Living Waters Program* as I shared in **My Story – Part Two**). Contact: Visit www.desertstream.org/group to find a *Living Waters Program* near you.
His Wonderful Works P.O. Box 81943 Conyers, GA 30013	Non-licensed Christian counseling and healing prayers – seeking the Lord's presence and power to meet our deepest needs for healing and wholeness. Contact: Visit www.hiswonderfulworks.com and go to Contact. Also, please go to Resources for additional support/help.
Restored Hope Network P.O. Box 64588 Colorado Springs, CO 80962	An interdenominational membership governed network dedicated to restoring hope to those bound to the old man through sexual and relational sin. Contact: Visit restoredhopenetwork.org and go to Find Help for support/help.

SUGGESTED READING

Bevere, John. *Breaking Intimidation* (Lake Mary, Florida: Charisma House, 1995).

Frangipane, Francis. *The Power of One Christlike Life* (New Kensington, Pennsylvania: Whitaker House, 2000).

MacArthur, John. *The Vanishing Conscience* (Nashville, Tennessee: Nelson Books, 1995).

Meyer, Joyce. *Battleground of the Mind* (New York, New York: Warner Faith, 1995).

Missler, Chuck and Nancy. *Be Ye Transformed* (Coeur d'Alene, Idaho: King's High Way Ministries, 1996).

Naselli, David and J.D. Crowley. *Conscience: What It Is, How to Train It, and Loving Those Who Differ* (Wheaton, Illinois: Crossway, 2016).

Payne, Leanne. *The Broken Image* (Grand Rapids, Michigan: Hamewith Books, 1996).

Payne, Leanne. *The Healing Presence* (Grand Rapids, Michigan: Hamewith Books, 1995).

Perkins, Bill. *When Good Men Get Angry* (Carol Stream, Illinois: Tyndale House Publishers, Inc., 2009).

Renner, Rick. *Sparkling Gems From the Greek* (Tulsa, Oklahoma: Teach All Nations, 2003).

Shreve, Mike. *65 Promises from God for your Child – Powerful Prayers for Supernatural Results* (Lake Mary, Florida: Charisma House, 2013).

Thomas, W. Ian. *The Indwelling Life of Christ: All of Him in All of Me* (Colorado Springs, Colorado: Multnomah Books, 2006).

ENDNOTES

Chapter 1

1. *Be Ye Transformed*, Chuck and Nancy Missler, © Copyright 1996 by Nancy Missler, thirteenth printing, April, 2016, Published by The King's High Way Ministries, Inc., Coeur d'Alene ID 83816. All rights reserved. Page 216.

2. "ingrained." Oxford Dictionary of English. © 2020 MobiSystems, Inc.

Chapter 2

1. "deep-seated." © 2012 Merriam-Webster, Inc. (15 June 2019).

2. "defiance." © Dictionary.com, LLC 2017.

3. "deep-seated." © 2012 Merriam-Webster, Inc. (15 June 2019).

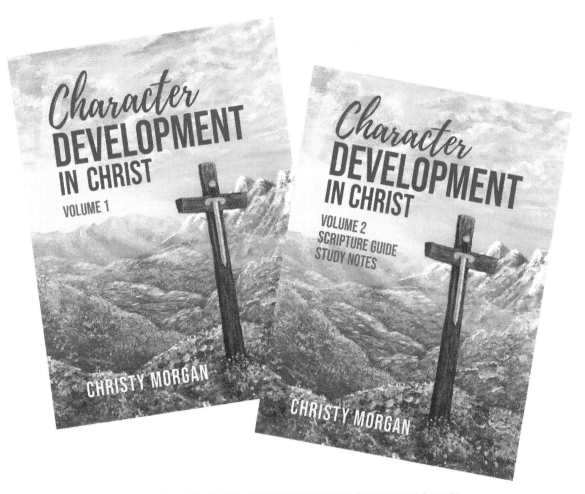

"CHRISTY MORGAN'S CHARACTER DEVELOPMENT IN CHRIST IS AN "OFF THE CHARTS" RESOURCE TO HELP BRING BREAKTHROUGH FOR EVERY BORN-AGAIN BELIEVER..."
—**Deanne "Dee" Barnes**, Founder, His Wonderful Works, Inc., CEO, Evans Tool & Die, Inc.

"IT IS IMPORTANT THAT CHRISTIANS BUILD A SCRIPTURE BASED FOUNDATION SO THAT OUR FAITH IS UNSHAKEABLE. WAY TOO OFTEN BELIEVERS ARE TOLD TO READ THE BIBLE. MANY HAVE TRIED AND FAILED HAVING HAD NO DIRECTION IN THEIR STUDIES. THE SCRIPTURE GUIDE STUDY NOTES, THIS SUPPLEMENTAL BOOK FOR CHARACTER DEVELOPMENT IN CHRIST, PROVIDES A PRACTICAL, SCRIPTURAL GUIDE TO BUILDING A BIBLICAL FOUNDATION. THE NOTES WALK YOU THROUGH THE SCRIPTURES THAT BRING HEALING AND MATURITY IN CHRIST."
—**Eddie Mason**, Senior Pastor, Southside Christian Fellowship Church

Available on Amazon!

Made in the USA
Columbia, SC
19 June 2023